FINDING FATHER

FINDING FATHER

STORIES FROM MENNONITE DAUGHTERS

EDITED BY
MARY ANN LOEWEN

University of Regina Press

Printed and bound in Canada at Friesens. The text of this book is printed on 100%
post-consumer recycled paper with earth-friendly vegetable-based inks.

Cover design: Duncan Campbell, University of Regina Press
Text design: John van der Woude, JVDW Designs
Copy editor: Alison Jacques
Proofreader: Kristine Douaud
Cover art: "Vintage Car Bench Seats" by Tim Newnman / iStockphoto.

Library and Archives Canada Cataloguing in Publication

Title: Finding father : stories from Mennonite daughters / edited by Mary Ann Loewen.
Other titles: Finding father (2019)
Names: Loewen, Mary Ann, 1956- editor.
Identifiers: Canadiana (print) 20189067969 | Canadiana (ebook) 20189067977 |
   ISBN 9780889775909 (softcover) | ISBN 9780889775916 (PDF) | ISBN
   9780889775923 (HTML)
Subjects: LCSH: Mennonites—Biography. | LCSH: Fatherhood—Religious aspects—
   Mennonites. | LCSH: Mennonites—Family relationships. | LCSH: Fathers and
   daughters. | LCGFT: Biographies.
Classification: LCC BX8141 .F56 2019 | DDC 289.7092/2—dc23

10 9 8 7 6 5 4 3 2 1

University of Regina Press, University of Regina
Regina, Saskatchewan, Canada, S4S 0A2
tel: (306) 585-4758 fax: (306) 585-4699
web: www.uofrpress.ca

We acknowledge the support of the Canada Council for the Arts for our publishing
program. We acknowledge the financial support of the Government of Canada. /
Nous reconnaissons l'appui financier du gouvernement du Canada. This publication
was made possible with support from Creative Saskatchewan's Book Publishing
Production Grant Program.

This book is dedicated to all who believe in the power of personal story, especially to those who are brave enough to tell theirs. And to Remy, part of the next generation of storytellers.

CONTENTS

Introduction *by Mary Ann Loewen*   ix

The Father Character *by Carrie Snyder*   1

"The Revery Alone Will Do" *by Rebecca Plett*   11

Requiem in Three Voices
by Ruth Loewen, Mary Ann Loewen, and Lynda Loewen   19

Finding My Father *by Cari Penner*   31

Technologies of Affection *by Ann Hostetler*   41

Seven Times with My Father *by Magdalene Redekop*   57

Go For It: Writing My Father's Story *by Julia Spicher Kasdorf*   69

Reflections of a Grateful Daughter *by Carol Dyck*   79

Our Lives Together, My Father and Me *by Hildi Froese Tiessen*   89

Journey *by Jean Janzen*   103

The Reluctant Farmer *by Maggie Dyck*   113

My Father and the Pieties *by Raylene Hinz-Penner*   127

Memoried with the Feel *by Elsie K. Neufeld*   137

Contributor Biographies   163

INTRODUCTION

*by **Mary Ann Loewen***

Car rides figure prominently in this collection of stories by Mennonite women of varying ages, places of birth, and social stations and from disparate places across Canada and the United States. These car rides have fathers driving daughters to school, to relatives' houses in the countryside, to work-related places. In this small, physical space on wheels, daughters and fathers spend uninterrupted time with each other. While not all the daughters experience a warm and reciprocal relationship with their father, the fundamental desire for that closeness beats at the heart of each of these stories.

This anthology features stories by Mennonite women about their fathers and, more specifically, stories about their relationships with their fathers. In *Sons and Mothers*, this book's companion piece, Mennonite men wrote about their mothers. These two collections taken together explore the cross-gendered mother-son and father-daughter relationships within a Mennonite context. And despite the emphasis on a particular ethnoreligious group, the stories in these collections have the potential to speak to parent-child relationships more universally—relationships that lie at the heart of all families. Given that these writers are Mennonites, these relationships are also shaped by other cultural artifacts, such as religion, minority status, and immigrant group experience.

The women in this book speak simultaneously in poetic and realistic terms about physical touch, faith, emotional accessibility, personality traits, professional achievement, and a desire to "please Father." They share candidly with the reader their desire for physical affection: "I see my father holding my hand, always holding my hand," writes Raylene Hinz-Penner in her chapter, and Magalene Redekop says that "It may be that I cherish the memory of that spot of warmth on my cheek because it was the last time I ever touched my father." These women share their encounters with fathers who are elderly and ill. Ann Hostetler writes, "His body is tensed and rigid, his eyes fearful, his presence urgent. 'Just breathe deeply,' I tell him." The women describe problematic characteristics they share with their fathers, as Julia Spicher Kasdorf's story demonstrates: "I could, I think, read his moods with clarity and his weapons of conflict with accuracy. They were and are, after all, my weapons as well." These examples point to the myriad ways these women become vulnerable in the space of this book, opening themselves up to the reader.

Life writing has become both popular and legitimatized in the last several decades. Many scholars have attested to its underlying authenticity, including John Paul Eakin, Sidonie Smith and Julia Watson, and Marlene Kadar, to mention but a few. But even those who believe in the significance of life writing—scholars like Bronwyn Williams, for instance—write that "reading creative nonfiction makes me...cringe...[because of] what the writers reveal about others" (296). Williams asks difficult questions of himself: "Who is implicated in the shaky memories I write about?...Whose story am I allowed to tell?" (297). Indeed, how do we who engage in this kind of writing negotiate the politics around it? Surely when we make public what was once private, we necessarily involve others. As Eakin asks, "How do we sort out the legitimacy of life writing...[and] specify its responsibilities...[when] the lives of others are centrally implicated in the telling of any life story?" (157). Personal writing is, after all, inherently political.

Certainly access to the secrets and subtleties of family dynamics plays an important role in this kind of writing. When Roxanne Coady, host of the podcast *Just the Right Book*, asked writer Ann Patchett about including actual family events and people in her latest novel, *Commonwealth*, Patchett replied, "Now, [at age forty-nine,] I want to have full access to my life...and that means that I'm going to be talking about some aspects of...[my family's] lives—because we overlap, but you know what? I'm entitled." I feel the same way Patchett does. I also want full access to my life, meaning that details of my life and the lives of those close to me will show up in public space someplace, sometime. And it also means that I want the writers in this collection to be allowed that kind of access.

The way to avoid hurting others in this process is by exercising what Margaret Somerville calls a "moral intuition," an intuition that to my mind is inextricably linked to respect and compassion (2). And if these approaches are the heart of our narratives, we will neither air dirty laundry for the sake of doing so, nor will we have to worry about denying ourselves "full access" to our stories. When personal writing is embarked upon from the premise of respect, it makes for a careful undertaking, a considered and considerate exploration. It is a form of writing that is conscious of its dangerous potential to dramatize, to serve as personal vindication, to exploit "the other."

Cari Penner had a hard story to tell, but because she undergirds it with tenderness, with understanding and respect, the access she employs serves to present to the reader an authentic person without disrespecting her father: "Ultimately, I did not find what I was searching for. I discovered, instead, something that I had never thought to find: a human being simply trying to be the best husband and father he could be." My sisters, Lynda Loewen and Ruth Loewen, and I also struggled with a father who, although hugely supportive of our educational pursuits and a good provider, seemed not especially interested in cultivating a close relationship with us. Ruth says, "I would never have said I was close to my dad. I never told him personal things or confided in him"; Lynda acknowledges that "my dad was not always the man I needed him to be"; and I recognize that "while he always liked to see my report card and often came to hear me play piano at the music festival,...I wasn't really part of his world." My sisters and I acknowledge an occasional glimpse into a slightly softer side to our father, but before his stroke in 1994 that side was difficult to access. But we three temper our stories with memories of Dad after his stroke, when he became warm and relational in ways he had not been before, in an effort to "balance the books."

Exploring the pasts of these men also helps the women writers make sense of their fathers' lives and attitudes. While some stories speak of carefree days spent on farms, often these stories represent times and places that compelled innocent young males to abruptly enter adulthood. Elsie K. Neufeld writes that her father "said the Allies were no better than the Germans, that the prisoners were herded, like animals, onto a field encircled with barbed wire, with armed guards watching from stations overhead." Some stories, such as Spicher Kasdorf's, recount young, conservative schoolboys at the cruel mercy of their more worldly peers: "Classmates threw his black felt Sunday hat down the hole in the outhouse, and non-Amish people yelled 'Conchie' and threw rotten tomatoes at his father." There are stories of fleeing war-torn Russia: of Hildi Froese Tiessen's father, for example, "leaving his home in the small village of Schöneberg…[and] waiting…while his parents made one last, hasty, heart-shattering stop at their own parents' homes, to utter their last farewells." Some stories are recountings of bitter tragedy: wives dying in childbirth, siblings drowning in watering troughs.

And there are stories of how grinding poverty left an imprint on the lives of these men and their daughters. The scholar Bill Roorbach encourages writers to "tell whatever story you have to tell exactly and truly, [despite] 'the urge to protect people in your life.'"* The women in this book implicitly heed such counsel; they share with the reader the inevitable chaos that results from living with many siblings in needy circumstances and how that chaos translates into emotional dysfunction as a father. Old tragedies announce themselves across generations. Certainly not all of the daughters' stories are happy ones.

In almost all of the memories recalled, the reader senses that these women have a particular relationship with their fathers. The daughters seem to hold their fathers to a different standard than they do their mothers, and they appear to love their fathers in ways they do not love their mothers. Certainly, many of them seem to *adore* their fathers. Carol Dyck writes that "whatever his shortcomings as a father may have been, he was kind and I loved him, and because of that, I was willing to forgive him for almost

---

* Quoted in Lynn K. Bloom, "Living to Tell the Tale: The Complicated Ethics of Creative Nonfiction," *College English* 65, no. 3 (2003): 278.

anything"; in contrast, Spicher Kasdorf's mother was "the taken-for-granted presence in the house." Are these women seemingly easier on their fathers because they secretly compete with their mothers for their fathers' attention? Do they love their fathers quite simply because they sense that it is the male who is their "ticket" out of a life of domesticity? For whatever reason, the cross-gendered factor plays prominently in the daughters' perceptions of, and longing toward, their fathers.

And while many of the writers admit that their fathers were products of an era of overt patriarchy—purchasing cars or planning family trips without consulting their wives, or referring to the women who worked for them as "the girls"—most of the daughters represent their fathers as surprisingly fair in a gendered world. This paternal veneration is especially apparent in stories in which fathers strongly encourage daughters to procure a college education, often ignoring the conservative religious and cultural expectations of the day. These men knew and applauded their daughters' intelligence. Many of these fathers had left the farm and become educated beyond their country school years, and they seemed to want the same thing for their children, regardless of their gender. Maggie Dyck writes that despite her parents' poverty, "education was of paramount importance [to them]..., second only to their faith." But sometimes this fatherly push for education came with an ambitious drive that was not always easily understood or necessarily welcome. Certainly, the women in this collection tell nuanced stories of their fathers, many well loved, all thoroughly scrutinized.

The connection that these women seek with their fathers is also expressed in accounts of stirring conversations they have with their fathers about "big ideas." These moments of closeness come during regular evening walks with their fathers, or as they accompany them on research or business trips. But even the happiest stories contain moments of conflict, disagreement, unfulfilled desires. Remembering a father's disappointment in a school grade, recalling unfair discipline at his hand, feeling frustrated at the inability to connect—the daughters present fathers who were neither only good nor only bad. They reveal a perceptive grasp of the complexity of these men and attest to novelist Elizabeth Strout's assertion that "whenever you've got people, nothing is simple." Indeed, these stories are embedded in nuanced sentiment.

Of course a book about Mennonite men, by Mennonite women, is also a book about religion. These stories reverberate with the negative impact that legalistic religious doctrine had on many of these men. Although there are exceptions, time and time again these women laud their fathers for refusing to manipulate them into the faith. Many of their fathers in fact disparaged fear as a means of procuring religious conformity. In addition, the majority of the women say that religion was assumed within the home, that faith was lived out in everyday life, but it was not talked about personally. These women describe how their fathers' integrity served as the fruit of their faith: "Dad lived, not spoke, his faith," writes Neufeld. Enough of the stories acknowledge this kind of religious openness so as to constitute a pattern, conditioned by the time and place in which these families lived. Often these women suggest that whether they remained active within a church setting was conditioned in some way by their relationships with their fathers.

For some of these writers, the father's character was less that of a close companion than that of the good man, a fair, decent provider, someone who represented the solid framework of the household, as Froese Tiessen points out, "less a force with whom I actively interacted than the environment, the matrix, in which I grew up." But for one daughter in particular, the father figure is neither her companion nor her champion, nor did she feel "counted" in his presence. The deepest tragedies occur when fathers are unable to give their daughters what they feel they need; these real-life situations are explored with gut-wrenching honesty and perceptible desire.

These stories might well have been different if they had been written fifteen, twenty years earlier. All life stories are coloured by time, by personal context. Indeed, Williams says, "there is no such thing as the 'truth'....[W]e all construct our perceptions and memories based on our experiences, our desires, our cultural expectations" (298). Yet these stories are no less "true" today than they would have been in the past. Surely experiences of illness and death soften the palette for at least parts of every story, but "the elegiac or sweetly nostalgic," as Rebecca Plett so beautifully enunciates, "which distance facilitates," although dangerous, is also authentic if the last memories a daughter has of her father are of his physical, and possibly mental, deterioration. If he has become a man other than what he was when the daughter was five, fifteen, thirty, even forty years of age. Indeed, a number of the writers recall the bittersweet time spent with their fathers as they neared their end. Jean Janzen, in fact, begins her story with her father's death: "He is tossing and turning. I caress him, this wonderful man, Henry Peter Wiebe, whom I adored all my life, try to calm him." Carol Dyck confesses that "the last years of my father's life were heavy and dark. Those painful last impressions of him are often still very vivid for me." The desire to allow sentiment to cloud our eyes is there, but the real story includes not only the latter days or years of a man's life, but also the writer's heartfelt response to that part of her father's life.

Many other themes—music, food, and humour, even complex issues like depression and redemption—are intricately woven into these pieces and help to make the fathers "come to life." Readers will find a variety of subjects and issues described, explored, and interrogated in these multi-layered narratives. But one more matter deserves specific recognition. A number of pieces allude to sexuality in some form or another, with references to fathers being aware of first menstrual periods and to embarrassing doctors' appointments with young male interns. Another story, which tells of sexual preference being announced, speaks candidly of "the betrayals of [the] body...[and] the dawning self-revelation of queerness" and describes this writer's prairie-born and -bred father's emotionally charged response to her "coming out."

This collection, then, includes difficult insights and memories, from the fear of not belonging to being unable to cry at a father's funeral. It also includes sanguine memories: "This is a love story. It's about a daughter loving, and being loved by, a father." The writers' inclination to "tell a real story" is to be lauded. Indeed, without the willingness to acknowledge the complicatedness of "a life," there is no story. So while many of these accounts are artistic, aesthetic gems, these women also weave a realistic tale of their lives with their fathers. The critics who write about personal narrative acknowledge the shifting sands on which we stand when we participate in this kind of writing. They also attest to the fact that all life stories necessarily reflect a fundamental relational dimension. Car rides, with father and daughter seated side by side, certainly mirror that interpersonal element. So when Eakin proposes that "the lives of others...[are]

implicated in the telling of...[our] life story" (157), I respond with, "and that is a good thing." It means we matter to others and they matter to us. This is a book about *mattering*.

> *We are in the car. Dad driving, both of us talking, holding cups of coffee....*
> *We use our wrists as shock absorbers as we fly over the railroad tracks....I*
> *ask Dad what we'd do with our cups if we were to get into a car accident—*
> *would we try to chuck them out the window? And he laughs and says he's*
> *wondered the same thing.* (Carrie Snyder)

WORKS CITED

Bloom, Lynn K. "Living to Tell the Tale: The Complicated Ethics of Creative Nonfiction." *College English* 65, no. 3 (2003): 276–89.

Eakin, John Paul. *How Our Lives Become Stories: Making Selves.* Ithaca, NY: Cornell University Press, 1999.

Loewen, Mary Ann, ed. *Sons and Mothers: Stories from Mennonite Men.* Regina: University of Regina Press, 2015.

Patchett, Ann. Interview by Roxanne Coady. "Ann Patchett on Humor, Heartbreak & *Commonwealth.*" *Just the Right Book*, podcast, March 30, 2017. http://www.bookpodcast.com/ep-19-ann-patchett-interview/.

Somerville, Margaret. *The Ethical Imagination: Journeys of the Human Spirit.* Toronto: House of Anansi Press, 2006.

Strout, Elizabeth. Interview by Roxanne Coady. "Elizabeth Strout Knows 'Anything Is Possible.'" *Just the Right Book*, podcast, July 26, 2017. http://www.bookpodcast.com/ep-36-elizabeth-strout-knows-anything-is-possible/.

Williams, Bronwyn. "Never Let Truth Stand in the Way of a Good Story: A Work for Three Voices." *College English* 65, no. 3 (2003): 290–304.

THE FATHER CHARACTER

*by **Carrie Snyder***

There is a particular photo that I'm thinking of now. We are new to each other, my dad and I; we have known each other no more than a few months. My dad proudly holds me aloft: an infant standing in the palm of his hand, my legs freakishly strong, my spine erect. I perform like a miniature circus act as he extends his arm to show off our trick to the camera. We both glow with delight, my face scrawny and rashy and his gap-toothed and bearded.

I have the flaming red hair that came from his grandmother.

These early hours and days and months are known to me through photographs, their colours garish with the hues and textures of the 1970s: baby Carrie florid in a scratchy orange-checked dress against a backdrop of paisley and corduroy. Note: redheads are not flattered by orange-checked dresses.

My dad's nickname for me, as a small child, was "Grunion." I looked it up in the dictionary once. It is a kind of fish. But he didn't choose the word for the meaning; it was the sound that summed me up, somehow, just like my brother Christian was "Grumbuff" (he really was).

I am writing the literary equivalent of a scrapbook. This will never do.

Memories flood in, good memories, but as I write them down, I alter them and their power diminishes, pinned to the page like a collection of dead butterflies; that is what I fear, although I am a writer, although writing things down is precisely what I've trained for and practised for all of my life, a claim that is scarcely hyperbole. At seven years old, I read in the *Guinness Book of World Records* that the youngest published author was a poet, a prodigiously talented four-year-old, news that came as a terrible shock—already past my prime!—and my dad humoured my sincere dismay, perhaps even encouraged it. It marked me as precocious, after all. Lost world records notwithstanding, he encouraged me—both of my parents encouraged me—to believe that I had the talent, the imagination, the intelligence to track down any goal, no matter how far-fetched. My mother believed (and still does) that her children are so fantastically gifted that her belief itself is fantastical, while my father balanced this out by believing that we could have done better. At seventeen, I showed him a term paper written for a third-year-level university history course, for which I'd received an A+; my dad read my paper and said he wouldn't have given it that mark, as it wasn't deserved. I was stung and furious. I also thought he was probably right.

Memories flood in, good ones, and yet I am writing about this grudge kept and nurtured for more than half my life. Good grief.

Perhaps it is the subject itself—my dad—that is tapping into insecurities like rotten roots, anxiety about my talents and the (diminishing?) powers of my brain, and, just as snarled, my doubts about this profession and its audacity to claim authority.

I want this essay to *please* my dad, as in, to meet his standards—yes, that is a piece of it—but also to please by giving him pleasure, to surprise and delight him.

⁕—⁕

We are in the car.

Dad driving, both of us talking, holding cups of coffee—actual coffee cups, no lids. The drive to the private Mennonite high school I attend as a grade nine student takes about half an hour from our home on the farm, and we leave at 7:40 in the morning. We use our wrists as shock absorbers as we fly over the railroad tracks in the valley. I ask Dad what we'd do with our cups if we were to get into a car accident—would we try to chuck them out the window? And he laughs and says he's wondered the same thing.

We listen to the news on the CBC.

For road trips, Dad makes the best sandwiches, their secret an everlasting mystery—what does he put in them? Is it the butter, thickly slathered? The thick layers of thinly sliced meat? I'll never be able to recreate those sandwiches.

Once, just before crossing into the States, Dad and I stop to buy fruit from a roadside stand to eat on the drive; at the border, the guard informs us that we will have to surrender our Canadian plums and peaches. Dad is so infuriated by the arbitrary stupidity of the demand that he angrily eats several peaches, juice dripping down his arm, while the border guard observes impassively from his little booth. Dad urges me to do the same, but I demur, somewhat diminishing his stand.

My dad is a quiet man, in many ways—shy, I think, with a complicated past that doesn't always make sense. I once wrote him as a character into a story only to have the editor return it with the remark, "This doesn't sound very plausible." The plot twist in question was when the character (i.e., Dad), a hippie bar musician with a fondness for soft drugs who has moved to Canada to avoid the draft, goes back to school and earns his PhD in Anabaptist history and becomes a respected scholar and beloved professor. I can see now why the editor said that. It *doesn't* sound very plausible.

My dad was also a peace activist who moved his young family to a country at war; he worked on farms, driving tractors and slopping hogs; he helped build silos as a teenager; he flunked out of Princeton, also as a teenager; he married very young and divorced, a secret that was kept from his children (i.e., us), the product of his second marriage, for years; the son and grandson of missionaries, he grew up speaking Spanish; he played bluesy songs on the piano, the soundtrack to my childhood, although he never learned how to read music; he taught Peace and Conflict Studies, yet his divorce from my mom, after thirty-four years of marriage, was marked by extreme acrimony.

In short, Dad is a person of contradictions. Aren't we all?

"Wouldn't it be great if parents were perfect, if parents made no mistakes," he once said to me, in a moment of sadness, when we were arguing, I think, although arguing is far too strong a word—we were not at peace with each other, we were struggling to see the other's point of view, we were hurt and bewildered and trying to meet up somewhere, anywhere.

I write fiction, and in my books and stories I've not yet managed to write a father character who satisfies me. This troubles me, but there it is. The fathers I've written have been absent, or silent, or charming and narcissistic, or even violent, at best bewildered, at worst destructive—always inadequate, not only as fathers but also as characters. I can't explain this problem, and it pains me. Does my failure to write strong fatherly characters imply a hollowness in my relationship with my own father? Does it reveal a lack between us? I fear this, but I refuse to believe it.

I know my dad.

But when asked to describe a father, my mind travels to clichés. I am pint-sized, looking up at a generic father who has a beard, a deep voice, who is powerful in some unnamed but slightly frightening way, who is irritated by our noise and play, who wants to be left alone, around whom we must sneak and from whom we must hide, in order to have our fun. His life is separate from his children's, fundamentally, fatally, as if he lives in a different world altogether, as if he is foreign to us and we to him, as if we can't see the extension of a deeper self in the other.

This is not my dad, this is an amalgam of dads I have known, or dads I remember knowing, which probably also includes fictional dads. I've read a lot of books. (Where, in the preceding set of clichés, is the version of the father with whom the child feels safe and protected?)

The real father, my dad, is too complex to be pinned down. During my childhood, he was a disciplinarian, sometimes stricter than our mom, but sometimes calmer. When I was a teenager, he tried to pay attention, to ask the right questions, to listen, but he couldn't help judging my choices, which shut down my answers, sometimes. And as an adult I worried about disappointing him by leading a traditional life, getting married relatively young, having four children, when perhaps he would have wanted for me a more cerebral existence, a life as an academic, which I did not turn out to be, despite striving to be for many years.

My dad grew up without a dad; he had no model for the role. If my dad were a fiction writer, it would be perfectly acceptable for him to write empty, hollowed-out father figures or golden fantasy father figures. His father died suddenly, of a cerebral hemorrhage, when my dad was nine months old. And so my dad was raised by a single mother.

Did he worry about becoming a father himself, about fulfilling the role? Did he wonder whether he was doing it right, with nothing to compare his own efforts against? Dad's mother was a high-energy, efficient, steely woman, who had no tolerance for the chaos caused by little boys; I cannot imagine what her sex education would have consisted of. She sent her teenaged son away to a private boys' boarding school. She rescued him, from time to time, or tried to. Her methods would not have been particularly gentle, I think. She is still alive, mellower now in her mid-nineties, but nevertheless fired by the same remarkable energy and drive.

In that regard, my dad doesn't take after his mother.

He is fond of naps.

He works steadily and patiently on projects that require a long devotion; he's said that he could have been a monk, bent over the pages of a book in perpetuity, and I believe it. And yet he is an amiable social creature and always has been. Even when my parents' marriage was fraying, they kept a welcoming house with an open front door—feeding their children's friends, hosting visitors from afar, making meals for colleagues and students and acquaintances. For years, they billeted international students or took in teenaged boarders, extra bodies in a house already filled to the rafters. I am the eldest of five children. Our house was never quiet, nothing like a monastery.

On Sundays, when we were all still attending church, Dad would stand in the front hall hollering that it was time to leave: we were going to be late! The scene would inevitably escalate as we dawdled and looked for earrings and pants and lost boots. Dad would threaten to go out to the car and start honking the horn. The front door would slam shut, and the car horn would indeed begin to honk, a rather distant sound, if you were still in the bathroom applying mascara. After some little while, the horn would go quiet. The front door would crash open. Dad, hollering, hopelessly, helplessly, comically: "Couldn't you hear me honking?"

We were always late for church.

I think of the futility and humour in that scene. Did Dad feel like he was dragging us all along behind him—our heavy unwilling bodies—expending a level of energy impossible to sustain, trying to ensure that we were raised as good Mennonite children in the tradition of his forefathers and -mothers? And is he disappointed, now, that none of us are regular churchgoers, not a one?

My dad is a man of faith. He comes from a long line of missionaries, but he is not an evangelist by nature. He has never tried to sway or persuade or pressure me into believing what he believes; instead, he has tried to show me by his actions, or to open a conversation. Like all good teachers, he asks questions and he listens to the answers with interest and curiosity, without judgment, even if he does not agree. I learned that skill from him.

❧ ⸺ ☙

There is a story I want particularly to tell.

On the Sunday after September 11, 2001, I went to church with my husband, who is not a Mennonite, and our baby boy, then four months old. We drove half an hour to come to the church, which my dad still attended, alone, as he had for a number of years.

My dad was preaching.

I remember where I was sitting, in a wooden pew with long maroon cushions on the right-hand side of the large, bright sanctuary. I remember that the church was packed full. People were searching for answers, for comfort in the face of terrifying images—of airplanes flown as weapons, skyscrapers falling down, dust and death and destruction, and the drumbeat of war. And I remember what my dad said. He stood at the pulpit and *he was himself*, so perfectly, that I will never forget it. He stood before us, mirroring our grief and bewilderment, asking our questions. He said that he did not know what to say. He said that the image that haunted him most, and he could not say why, were the people who had been trapped at the tops of those buildings, unable to escape, choosing to jump.

He said, "I can't stop thinking about them."

And then he opened the Bible and read to us from the Sermon on the Mount. He told us that reading it had given him comfort. He shared that comfort with us in a manner that was simple, straightforward, grief-stricken, and honest. What I'm certain we were witnessing was the power of vulnerability and the power of truth, a mirror for our grief, reflected through my dad.

I will remember that moment always.

Afterward, people crowded to thank him with tears in their eyes. They wanted to hold his hands and tell him how much what he'd said had meant to them. I tried to tell him, too, how profound his gift was, in that moment, but words failed me. Dad wouldn't take credit for what he'd done. *Don't thank me, thank a higher power.*

I would call that power grace. My dad might call it God, or the Holy Spirit.

This past fall, I took my daughter, Flora, who is eleven years old, to visit my dad and stepmom. Flora was working on a school project for which she needed to interview a relative who had come from another country, and she'd chosen Grandpa Arnold. I sat curled on the couch, my stepmom nearby in a reclining chair under a blanket, Flora very upright and professional in a straight-backed chair holding her notebook and pen, and Dad leaning back in a comfortable chair opposite us, taking time to consider Flora's questions. He told her about elementary school teachers he had liked and disliked and about animals he'd had as a child living in Puerto Rico (a pony, and a dog, though I noticed he skipped mentioning the pet rooster, which his mother killed for soup one day—a story that fascinated me as a child).

Flora was most excited to ask one particular question: "What was Mom like when she was little? Was she like me?"

My dad smiled at this. He was very relaxed and calm. "Enthusiastic," he said. "Your mom was always so enthusiastic and curious about everything."

The answer might have been for Flora, but it felt like a gift being given to me. In that instant, I saw my child-self through his eyes, and I saw how loved and cherished she was—I was; I am.

As the conversation wound down, Flora asked her last question: "What is one thing in the world you would change if you could?"

Dad sighed deeply. "Death," he said. "I would make it so no one would ever die." He looked at my stepmom and smiled with deep sadness, and she smiled back at him from across the room. She was wearing a knitted hat and drinking tea, preparing for another round of chemo to fight back the cancer that had settled in, terminally, we'd been told. We talked about Dad's idea for a little while. We didn't stop there, if you see what I'm saying; we questioned the concept, we had a conversation: we wondered whether a person would simply get older and older and never die, or whether a person would stay a certain age and never die—and would the world get too full? Would there be room for new people?—and in the end, my dad said he could see that it wasn't the most practical idea.

But he still wished for it.

Am I capturing him? Am I coming close?

I told him last week that I'd been asked to write this essay and that I still hadn't gotten started. "I've got lots of ideas and lots of scenes in my head, but I just can't seem to write them down," I said. "Something seems to be stopping me; I'm not sure what." He laughed and said that awhile back he'd been asked to write an essay on mothers and sons, but had refused. He didn't explain why, and he didn't need to: too complicated, where to begin? Even to begin with love does not seem sufficient.

"I have only good things to say," I said to Dad.

Of course, that is not completely true. And yet, it almost completely is. When I think of my dad, it's the good moments that flood my memory. The car rides, as I've said. The quiet conversations. The smell of rich food cooking—stacks of Swedish pancakes devoured on Saturday mornings with sugar and butter and syrup; spicy pasta sauce with hamburger; a rice dish with tomato sauce that we called "guiso," which we would eat hot and covered in melted cheese; countless pots of soup, vegetable-beef or potato or fish chowder; mashed potatoes loaded with cream cheese and butter. My dad cooks like we are farmers coming in from hard labour in the field.

Enough, I think. This is sufficient. I'm getting hungry, it's time for lunch.

But I've remembered one more scene, from a time that is almost now. A fresh scene in a story that I want to go on and on.

We are in the car.

My dad is driving me to an eye appointment in a nearby city. I can't drive myself, having injured my retina while playing in an indoor soccer game (the ball struck my head, very hard). So Dad has offered to drive, even though his life, at present, involves a great deal of waiting in waiting rooms to see medical professionals. It is snowing, the roads are slick, and my little car doesn't have snow tires, yet I feel perfectly safe.

We sit together in the waiting room. Dad has brought along a thick text written in German, which he'd ordered through the library system from New York City. There are only a few copies in existence in North America. "It looks like you're the first person to read that book, ever," I say. He recounts a funny story he's read in the book, and I try to laugh, but the lights are bright, the waiting room is crowded, and dreadful seasonal music blares from a speaker nearby, none of which helps my concussed head. I try to follow Dad's story, but it is from the sixteenth century and all I can hear is "*in the meadow, we can build a snowman...*"

Dad returns to the text. Every once in a while, he chuckles, amused by the words on the page. He is absolutely engrossed when I return, some long while later, from the warren of examination rooms behind the front desk, ready to go.

The retina is only bruised. I won't need surgery. Dad is thrilled. He doesn't tell me I should stop playing soccer, but he agrees with me when I suggest it myself. We drive home, not talking too much. We hug and say goodbye in the driveway. He has walked to our house, so he heads off down the snowy sidewalk, on foot.

I have no photos of us, together, as we are, now. I've only just thought of that.

I am in my early forties. My dad is seventy, but I believe he could move my piano for me, single-handedly, if I needed him to; that's how strong I think he is. Isn't that a lot of weight to put on a person? But isn't it true? He's listened, he's laboured, he's questioned, he's searched, he's learned. He asks wistful, whimsical questions, he wishes, he wonders, he allows that he doesn't know the answers. He is strong.

Of course, I am talking not only of the body now. I return to the image that returns.

Once, he held me in the palm of his hand.

"THE REVERY
ALONE WILL DO"*

by *Rebecca Plett*

W hen I was a baby, my parents bought a property straight south of the turkey farm where my father was born and raised. Our childhoods—my father's and mine—took place against the backdrop of abrupt changes from winter to summer and back again, the stark horizon line of the flat, flat prairie, the frenzy of the growing season. My father and I both grew up in the same square-mile section of southern Manitoba, both went to school at and graduated from Landmark Collegiate— though most of his grade school education was in a one-room schoolhouse in the tiny hamlet of Linden.

I left Landmark (or its more poetic iteration, Prairie Rose) after gradu-ation, like he did, for the grand metropolis of Winnipeg; we both went to Bible college (he to Mennonite Brethren Bible College [MBBC] and me to Canadian Mennonite Bible College [CMBC]) and then on to the hallowed

---

* Quoted from Emily Dickinson's poem "To make a prairie" (1755).

halls of the Universities of Winnipeg and Manitoba, respectively. We both found life and love in new connections with southern Ontario, but it's here where our stories part ways: he returned to stay on the Prairies, and I left for good, though my heart did not.

The sprawling concrete of Toronto reaches all the way to my Hamilton home, where steel factory smokestacks fill the air with a yellow smog whenever there is an east wind. Forests, waterfalls, and lakefront offer respite, though it pales, in my mind, to the relief of the vast prairie sky and the simplicity of that eternal horizon line. To love the prairie, I suppose, requires care for detail, to see, and to want to see, subtlety.

My father is, in my memory, imbricated with that prairie landscape, forming a symbiosis between biography and ecology. Like the broad plains of southeastern Manitoba, his character is subtle: he is not prone to wild swings in emotion, affect, volume, or language, but his complexity is there if you care to look. He himself is an observer, a collector of details, caring about looking and observing. I will occasionally get updates about the animals that make appearances in the stillness of my parents' rural property: there is a new fox family by the Hildebrands' barn; we have an owl nest in the shelterbelt; we heard coyotes the other evening. In his introversion, he is able to pay attention, to attune himself to the quality of quiet and to glean meaning and richness from it. Some may balk at this life, considering it small and confined; I suspect those who do might also be the types who speed through Manitoba and Saskatchewan on their way to mountain destinations, bored by the consistent landscape.

Amid the stillness, you can attend closely to things, make them familiar, understand the small but important gradients of change. This is particularly true of the landscape of the Prairies; those "pioneering" Mennonites settling onto the flatlands of southern Manitoba read the subtleties of acclivity enough to fashion a drainage system to mitigate the effects of the flooding river system. This familiarity and deep knowledge is, I think, a form of mediating those forces seemingly beyond human control—"in God's hands"—or those within the realm of human intervention. In microcosm, and in concert with this wider system, my dad goes out each spring to carve out tiny trenches with a triangle-shaped hoe to drain the pools of water, lest they overcome the sump pump and flood the basement.

My dad keeps order through attention to these small events, an extension of knowing what's happening as a means of control: marking the arrival of a new owl, knowing who is "driving on [his] road," having a repository of up-to-date knowledge of various Mennonite relationships, gossip, and current politics. He marks a difference, though, between knowing and learning, and he has drawn clear lines around things he does not want to learn: he somehow got the hang of boiling potatoes, but learning to cook pasta is a definite no. Sometimes it comes down to controlling the things he wants to know and, as a corollary, what others around him should know or want to experience.

Before this delves too deeply into the elegiac or sweetly nostalgic, which distance facilitates, I wish to state clearly that my father is all sides of a complex man: he can, at times, be petty, indifferent, taciturn, and silent. It is this silence that my mother has sometimes railed against. And though I do not recall openly fighting with my father, I could, I think, read his moods with clarity and his weapons of conflict with accuracy. They were and are, after all, my weapons as well.

My father is not a man of many words. In fact, my family likes to complain that his favourite word is a definitive "no," most often perceived as ruinous, a dampening of enthusiasm for a plan or idea. I think, though, that he's exercising caution in words and action, his "no" often being deployed as a space holder as he considers potential outcomes. But brevity is also not quite true of my father: he chats; he's a master at chatting. The mode of talking that draws out deep, emotional connection, however, did not always come easily, especially because my mother is a big proponent of *leaning in* to those tough and affective discourses, to gleaning the nooks and crannies of feeling, perhaps to the point of paying attention to *only* the crises.

My mother is also a very affectionate person, quick to hug and kiss; she loves to laugh and loves to prank—a consummate caregiver, now ending her career in palliative care. My father, in contrast, is reticent to hug (not that he doesn't want to, but rather thinks "why would anyone want a hug from *me*?" A telling statement in itself). He doesn't look people in the eye, and, as many of my friends have noted, it's difficult to assess whether he likes you or not. Though he never cared for machismo, force, or a raised voice in what I saw of his fathering, he does exude a sense of quiet power and authority and asserts his oldest-child position with ease. The emotive thoughts my father has, however—his feelings and desires—are often filtered through my mother. It is the times I'm alone with my mother that I hear about how much my dad enjoyed his last visit to Ontario, or the sadness he feels as they consider a move away from their rural property.

There is a tendency among Mennonites, as "people of the book," to put much stock in words, their authority, and a preference for directive over emotion. The way we use words or remain silent is given gendered meaning, where women are asked to achieve literacy in emotive discourse and men to speak without it. My parents seemed to fall into neat categories of feminine and masculine, and these categories were what I learned as a child. I felt, therefore, that repeated declarations (sometimes derisive) that I "was just like Dad" were meant to shame, to make me feel like a wet blanket and a killjoy, and, indeed, I internalized them that way. "I am warm!" I thought. "I can be spontaneous and fun, I hug, I care for people!" The discomfort I felt in this derision was that I, somehow, was being masculinized—that unlike the warm, caregiving women on my mother's side, I was cold, distant, and therefore "cerebral" like my father.

This created a series of conundrums for me as to the definitions of masculinities and femininities that we as Mennonites are socialized into: Is my father more "cerebral" because he doesn't always speak from the heart? Am I more "feminine" because I have come to be literate in a certain discourse and language in which I can articulate, reflect, and communicate my feelings, desires, needs, and wants? So how did I, a Plett raised in Landmark, going to school with my second and third Plett cousins (not to mention Reimers and Penners) in the same building from K through 12, end up doing a PhD in cultural anthropology? What was so alluring to me about feminism during my undergrad years? How did (the capture of?) the ideologies of social activism, justice, and anti-oppression come to my small corner of southern Manitoba?

Much credit goes to my mother, an outsider, and her push to leave the Evangelical Mennonite Church (EMC) Church and its hesitancy to recognize the leadership of women. She also consciously decided to earn her "own" money and was the only one of the mothers I knew to work outside the home. Her immigrant drive to earn, earn, earn, to work hard, and her Mennonite Brethren desire to show it all off was tempered, however, by my dad's EMC desire to keep quiet and not draw attention; this was sometimes a tension between them, but was sometimes neatly complementary.

My mother has a fiery, frisky side (like all of the Schmidt women on her mother's side—of whom there were many) that she channelled into relentless productivity. From her, I learned to see beyond my town and to be drawn to ideas from beyond its borders. And so, like many young Mennonites, I used words, ideas, literature as means to escape: the allure of feminism and the safety of the world of ideas pulled me along a lifelong academic path. My brother left our small town, too, though his move was based less on a sense of self-preservation than mine was. We both felt the pull of the world of ideas. Ironically, we both ended up in or near our mother's hometown of Kitchener, Ontario.

This is not to say, though, that university lent an immediate reprieve, or was some magic salve in opposition to the cliché of a repressive small-town life. For me, it also held within its walls a sense of transgression—that somehow, deep down, education was fraught; that it would lead to dangerous ideas that could threaten and collapse a way of life that was precious and enduring; that education could distill that life to meaninglessness and worldliness. This, after all, was at the heart of the Mennonite exodus out of Canada when the government asked for education in English. Sometimes I wonder if my forebears who came from Russia—my grandparents who pioneered in Paraguay and came to Canada as the pejorative "displaced persons"—would be disappointed at my embrace of worldliness, at my apathy toward the church, when their dedication to it, their culture, and God meant risking their lives.

The university was ultimately, for me, a place where diversity of bodies and of experience was lauded, welcomed, and discussed, and I was affirmed for my choices by my parents, and particularly by my father. He also has a graduate degree, and he openly admires the pursuance of education. Sometimes I think it comes even closer to adulation, listening to the authority of the PhD as near divine, and, in my opinion, often uncritically. It was during my own experience in graduate school that this granting of authority became problematic for me. I became sensitive to the displays of masculinity in academia that felt familiar to my own experience in small-town life—the obvious grabs for power, or the oblivion with which some men framed their privilege. My experience in academia has sensitized me, even in these modern times, to the power and entitlement white men take as a given: the higher likelihood of employment, the confidence with which they speak in public. The fact that they know they have a voice and are given it.

I suspect the way this particular aspect of academia (and elsewhere) gets under my skin like nothing else has something to do with where I grew up, in my small Mennonite town in rural Manitoba, the same one my father grew up in. While he was granted the privileges that white men hold in our context, he was sensitive to my protestations against them; though he was perhaps oblivious to these privileges, he listened with sensitivity when they were revealed.

Despite my education, my attentive father, and my determined mother, the narratives of matrimony, maternity, and subordination to men that signalled maturity and "correctness" held fast within, and though I can't recall their overt iteration, the rhizomes of such inculcation run deep within. Those roots are, apparently, nearly impossible to destroy, and the quack grass that sprouts from them pops up in the unlikeliest of places, sometimes under surprising circumstances. I was someone, after all, who was loath to be the centre of attention, never ever wanting to stand out—something I inherited from my father. How unfortunate for me (or so I felt) to experience the effects of puberty so acutely: I grew to a gangly six feet during high school and was featured prominently in the middle of the back row of every single class picture. It was mostly me and the boys in the back, while the smaller girls were posed demurely in the front. The terrible posture that has plagued me into my adult years is a reminder of the days I felt the betrayal of my body—something that, perhaps, many women feel in some form or another. I look back at pictures of my adolescent self and see that desire to fold up into myself: a lanky, awkward frame bookended by large feet and hands, hidden by oversized clothes (there were some blessings in early-nineties fashion).

The betrayals of my tall body were nothing, however, to my early years in university that brought with them the dawning self-revelation of queerness. Such was my horror at this prospect, and the surety of familial rejection, that I buried this secret deep, deep down in the recesses of my psyche. I won't ever speak of this to anyone, I declared at the time; I'm not meant to do this, to be so very different. This dissociative state between my body and mind was, of course, eventually incommensurable. And so I moved away, leaving for graduate school and anonymity. I relished the thought of moving to a city where I was the only Plett for miles around—or at least as far as Kitchener, where my brother was the only other one.

Time and space led to comfort in this body of mine, and the day arrived when it became necessary for me to tell my parents I was queer: I knew it in my very core, though I can't articulate why. The only problem was summoning the words, to form them on my lips, to, in my mind, risk everything in uttering two words: I'm gay. Every time I imagined how I might say it—confess it—hot bile came up into my throat instead of sound. How is it that the act of speech, of forming and vocalizing certain words, can elicit such a violent bodily reaction? Besides, what was it that I was so afraid of?

This is what I told myself as I flew, alone, to Winnipeg and then drove to my parents' house on a cold Christmas Eve. After dinner, I started crying, knowing it was now or never. And so, somehow, impossibly, I summoned forth the words "I am gay" from the pit of my stomach and the recesses of my psyche to face the harsh light of day. The words had barely formed in the air between us. I sat in shock—and still do—at the unfathomable scene, where my father, usually so reticent to touch, without hesitation rose from his chair across from me, moved around the table, and put his arms around me.

Sometimes I think about these wordless gestures, a surer indication of love and acceptance than any utterance, and how it was nearly impossible for me to form the words, to exclaim some sort of truth, to confess, as it were. And yet what I received was not a word, but a reflexive expression that communicated something far beyond my expectations, something vulnerable, something deeply parental. It came from the same place that it did when my dad sang to me when I was sick as a child. I had migraines, and the only relief from the intense pain was to lie still for hours on end. While I couldn't respond, let alone move, my dad would come into my room with his guitar and sing in his rich baritone—Simon and Garfunkel, Jim Croce, and Donovan—and then leave again.

In these gestures I came to understand, in part, how words and silences inform one another, the width and breadth of masculinity and femininity, and how we come to assign them all the meaning in the world when they are, at the same time, absolutely meaningless. I'll continue to work at how and when to reject these binaries from a queer perspective and when to allow them patience and space as ways to structure lives.

I have come to see my father as thoughtful, cerebral, but also affecting, able to access a language of meaning and feeling beyond words. It is a language he accesses more and more frequently, when now, more than ever, he allows himself the vulnerability. Perhaps it is a luxury of age, where there are fewer of the stresses of a young career and family, more self-assurance, and the increasing closeness of illness and death allow for closer contemplation and reflection. My father laughs and cries more than I remember in my childhood, moved by music and the trials and travails of life. Maybe this was always there, but in my haste to leave, I drove too fast and almost missed the complexity in that stark horizon line.

REQUIEM IN THREE VOICES

by *Ruth Loewen, Mary Ann Loewen, and Lynda Loewen*

Our father died in February of 2016 at the age of ninety-three. At his funeral each of his six children—three boys and three girls, as my dad liked to say—offered a tribute to him. These are the reflections (somewhat altered for this contribution) that we three daughters, in order of age, read aloud to the congregation.

1. RUTH

I would never have said I was close to my dad. I never told him personal things or confided in him, rarely asked for help or advice except occasionally about financial things. But looking back it's clear to me that I had a somewhat special relationship with him, one that was unique in our family. And it's also clear that some of Dad's early attempts to influence me did eventually have an effect, if only years later.

I was the eldest and therefore I got the full brunt of Dad's academic aspirations for his kids, which were considerable. Learning came fairly easily to me, at least through grade school, so he never had cause to lower his expectations of me. At the end of grade seven, I was one of only three students in my class to exceed an average of 75 percent in all subjects and therefore be exempted from all exams. However, Dad decided 80 percent was a more appropriate standard for his offspring, which meant I had to write three of my exams after all.

There was a later occasion when I got 97 percent on a test and Dad's response was, "What happened to the other 3 percent?" He was quite serious: three marks were not to be dispensed with lightly. I was quite annoyed. Why couldn't I have had a father who was pleased with 97 percent?

But Dad's standards must have rubbed off on me. Decades later, near the beginning of my master's degree, I went to my instructor with an assignment and asked, "What did I do wrong here? Why did I get an A and not an A+? I need to know how to improve." The instructor hardly knew how to answer me. Possibly no one had ever protested getting an A before.

Mum and Dad always enjoyed classical music, and I remember the night they brought home their first stereo system—what a wonder that wooden cabinet was! They also bought a set of light classical records that were played often over the years; there was no TV to compete with music at that stage of our family life. Those symphonies and operas have seemed like old friends to me all my life.

But I was a teenager during the early days of rock 'n' roll, and my dad didn't want me corrupted by this music. So he bribed me: if I didn't buy rock music, he'd buy me recordings of classical music. I know I sometimes still listened to rock music, and I did buy at least some popular music—in fact, I was astounded on a recent family vacation when my youngest siblings knew the words to my very first purchase, a tune called "Ooo, I Love Onions." But Dad's influence took effect. Now, when friends talk enthusiastically about any of today's music, I have to confess that classical music is the only genre I really like or understand at all.

Both our parents were extremely casual about physical safety. As far as I know, they never locked the doors of any house they lived in. Mum was in full agreement with this policy, but it probably sprang from Dad's upbringing. His parents' house was famous for having been locked on only one occasion: when an unexpected visitor found the house empty and decided to stay overnight on her own.

When our parents bought one of the nicest homes in Morris, Manitoba, they received a box containing thirteen keys. When they sold the house seven years later, they handed the box of keys to the new owners. Mum told me they had never even determined which key belonged to which door.

While they lived in that house, I came home from a year in Europe without warning, wanting to surprise them. A friend picked me up at the airport and drove me to their house in Morris. I was worried that they wouldn't be home, since they didn't know I was coming. I was relieved to see, as we approached, that lights were on in many rooms. But it turned out that they weren't at home after all; they were away for the weekend. Their idea of burglar-proofing the house was to leave all the lights on *instead* of locking the doors. At least I was able to wait for them inside the house.

Dad was also casual about the physical safety of his kids. During the time the family lived in Morris, when I was in university and my sister Mary Ann was in high school, the two of us decided on a day of shopping in Winnipeg. We took the bus from Morris, an hour's ride. But we missed the last bus home, so we phoned Dad at his office: "Dad, you're going to have to come pick us up in Winnipeg. We have no way to get home." We knew Dad didn't much like ferrying his family around, so maybe we should have anticipated his response: he told us to take a bus to the city limits and hitchhike to Morris from there. So that's what we did. Many years later when I told this story to a new friend, she exclaimed with horror, "You should have called *my* dad. He would have picked you up."

As the eldest daughter by five years, I was Mum's chief helper. She took my help for granted in day-to-day ways, like cleaning and cooking, but it was Dad who turned to me whenever he thought Mum was overwhelmed by a bigger responsibility, like a family event of some kind. When Mary Ann got engaged, I was thirty and living in Ontario. In most families it would be the mother of the bride who planned, or helped to plan, a wedding. But I guess Dad knew this would be too daunting for Mum, and so he paid for me to fly to Winnipeg to help get things organized. As it turned out, I didn't get to do much. When I asked Mary Ann about her plans, specifically about food preparation, she said "Why do we have to think about that now? There's still six weeks until the wedding."

Another of those daunting events occurred a decade or so later. It was Dad's turn to host the every-other-year gathering of his two siblings and their grown children, who were coming from the Maritimes and various parts of the United States. Preparing for this was a huge amount of work, partly because Dad and his siblings tended to compete with one another. Dad wanted the event to be held in Steinbach in his family's old home, which he'd purchased from his brother and sister. Preparing the house for numerous overnight guests required multiple trips between Steinbach and Winnipeg, the latter being where my parents were living then. Mum was almost literally pulling her hair out, trying to meet Dad's expectations. Once again Dad tried to solve the problem by asking for my assistance. He offered to pay my airfare if I'd take two weeks' vacation before the gathering, to help Mum with the preparation. This time I declined. I remember saying to a friend that it was a choice between guilt if I turned Dad down and resentment if I accepted his offer.

There were a couple of other occasions when Dad paid for me to fly home, expecting nothing of me except my presence. One of them was his retirement dinner when he left the Canadian Foodgrains Bank (CFGB). For financial reasons I had planned to not attend, but the event wasn't complete for Dad if I wasn't there. That time it was our little secret; he surprised the rest of the family by having me turn up at the last minute.

After Dad retired from the CFGB, he had more time for other interests, and he capitalized on that in surprising ways. He took a course in bread making and became an avid baker of breads, at a time when bread machines weren't yet available. And he started exercising regularly, both biking and going to the YMCA.

By coincidence I was also into baking bread at that time, and I had recently joined a fitness club. For the first time Dad and I had actual interests in common, something to talk about besides my paltry finances and my less paltry grades. We compared bread recipes and kneading techniques. And I still remember the time Dad and I were both lying on the carpeted floor of my apartment, demonstrating to each other the leg exercises that we had recently learned. It's a pity no one was around to immortalize that occasion with a photo.

After his retirement, Mum and Dad were happier together than I'd ever seen them. Dad was working part-time for Gardewine Transportation, a delivery company, drafting a policies and procedures manual, and Mum was able to help him with some of the writing. Part of Dad's job was to visit the various outposts of this company, to assess practices and morale. Those were just the kind of car jaunts that Mum liked; she was happy to accompany him all over the province. Theirs was a partnership at last. It was all the more tragic, therefore, that the following winter Dad had a severe stroke during open-heart surgery.

After his stroke, family dynamics changed utterly. Mum was forced to take responsibility for all their finances, and now she was the one who went around the house turning off lights—something I remember Dad doing when I was in high school. Mum had always been dependent on Dad, typical of women of her generation, and now he was completely dependent on her. But I was living in Ontario and of little use to either parent. They needed daily help, not an occasional visit. So they turned to my three youngest siblings, who were in Winnipeg and didn't yet have families of their own. I was off the hook as far as Dad's needs were concerned, permanently.

Everything I had shared with Dad, virtually our entire relationship, was wiped out, literally overnight. This was true for my siblings too, of course, but they lived in Manitoba and continued to interact with him regularly. He needed them and new relationships were created out of that dependence. Because I visited Winnipeg only once or twice a year, I didn't see enough of Dad to craft much of a new bond with him.

Dad didn't forget me, though. Occasionally he let me know that I was still on his radar. He liked to phone me, especially on my birthday. Once he called me at work to give me birthday greetings, but because he didn't know where in the university I worked, he had to talk to several people before he finally reached me on the phone. In the process he alerted my co-workers to the fact that it was my birthday, so I got far more greetings that year than any year before or since.

Even in Dad's final year, he would get his helper Wilf to dial my work number every now and then, and if I was in my office we'd have a sixty-second chat. He'd tell me about his workout that day—upper body or lower body; he alternated day by day. And he'd remind us both that the previous president of my university, David Johnston, was now the Governor General of Canada. He didn't really know what my job entailed, but he was sure it was worthwhile, so he was proud of me.

When I got the news that Dad had died, I realized I would never again hear him greet me. Because he was blind and also fairly deaf, I'd have to identify myself loudly—"Dad, it's Ruth"—and he'd say "RUTH!" with recognition and considerable pleasure in his voice. He never had much to say to me after that, but I knew he was happy I was there. I will miss that knowledge.

2. MARY ANN

Dad had a lot of personal agency in the first seventy-one years of his life; in the last twenty-two years he did not.

I grew up knowing my dad as someone who took charge of things. He was always in a position of leadership, as a high school teacher, a guidance counsellor, a school division administrator, or a pastor. He liked to succeed in all of his public challenges, and he was good at getting things done. And he did a lot of good things in his lifetime, including getting grain out to people who needed it in Africa. But it was not until I was an adult that I found out that not everyone appreciated these efforts of his. I learned that he sometimes bumped into people, that his drive to achieve the goals he set for himself sometimes met with disapproval from others. And while some of us would lose sleep over that kind of thing, my father did not. He slept soundly regardless of what others thought of him. He was, in some ways, a one-man show.

I was about ten, and I remember walking with my dad to Leoppky's Jewellers in Steinbach, Manitoba, two blocks from our house. We were going to buy my birthday gift, a recording of the Medical Mission Sisters singing their folksy, Christian songs: "I Cannot Come to the Banquet," "Joy Is like the Rain"—those songs. I remember talking to Dad about my mom as we walked, wanting to know why she was sometimes unhappy; I don't remember exactly what he said, but I'm pretty sure hormones came up as a plausible reason. I know that the situation between them was complicated, but I also think that he was sometimes genuinely confused as to why things were the way they were. In any case, the reason I remember this walk is because I didn't often spend time with Dad on my own. He was a good provider, he was kind to me, I'm sure he taught me a lot, and I trusted him. But I wasn't really close to him. While he always liked to see my report card and often came to hear me play piano at the music festival, I don't remember a lot of conversations with him. He was a mover and a shaker, and I wasn't really part of his world.

But then his stroke happened. On my daughter Rebecca's eleventh birthday, February 26, 1994, everything changed for him—and for the rest of us. After months of medical instability and general confusion, after frustrating uncertainty as to what he would have left to work with, my dad gradually emerged as a different person, in some very fundamental ways. Over time he became interested in what others were doing, even if those things didn't directly impact him. And those others included me. After his stroke, although my educational pursuits were still of special interest to him, he was now also interested in me as a person. He would ask me questions about my life; he really wanted to know how I was and what I was up to. He also became curious about my children—indeed, about all of his grandchildren. He wanted to know whatever it was they were involved in. And he cheered them on.

He also grew to appreciate compassion. In the last year or so, whenever I would leave him on Saturday evening, I would tenderly plant a kiss on his forehead; inevitably he would smile, maybe gently chuckle, and say, "Thank you for the kiss." I had another singular position within the family: whenever Dad got a haircut it was my job to notice and to comment on it. His haircuts, as you can imagine, were never drawn-out affairs (my father was mostly bald for most of his adult life), so you had to look closely to see that he had in fact visited a barber. My noticing these subtle cosmetic changes began when I was young, and the "job" stuck; in fact, just a month or so ago, I said to him, "Dad you got a haircut!" and he responded, "Yup, Mary Ann, you always notice that!" And I knew he was happy that I had.

The man who ran organizations, who led myriad meetings, who slept regardless of who thought what of him, now had to let others do for him. My mother ended up taking on a lot of the care for many years. I remember that when they lived in their condo on Henderson Highway, she set up a mat for herself on the hallway floor outside Dad's bedroom; she needed to hear him if he needed something at night. But she also got to control significant parts of his life. If she decided that Dad's daily allotment of Bothwell cheese was a mere square inch, well, then a square inch was his lot. And if she decided to take all the time in the world to finish her toast in the morning at Smitty's (and believe me, she was a slow eater to begin with!), as they ate together with Pinky or Kerry or Nathan or Wilf (his wonderful home care workers), well, then Dad just had to sit there and wait for her. He rarely complained, but I often wondered at this subtle shift in power.

Dad learned to be patient—exceedingly patient—and he increasingly learned how to relate to all kinds of people.

I was very sorry that he lost his sight and his spatial orientation, but in exchange he gained a spiritual vision and a groundedness that not only stood him well, but also allowed people like me to enter his life in meaningful ways. We all changed as a result of Dad's stroke, but he changed the most. He learned to love and accept all kinds of people; he welcomed everyone who entered our family, irrespective of their educational or religious backgrounds. He learned that wine and beer were not of the devil; we used to joke at Christmas gatherings that it didn't matter if he drank red or white wine—he couldn't see the difference, anyway. He learned that life was meant to be lived one day at a time; you might as well since you couldn't necessarily control the outcome. He also learned that humour ameliorates a lot of potentially difficult situations. A week ago the five of us went to see him. He was in bed at suppertime—an unusual state of affairs. He clearly was very weak. The nurse came in and turned on the bright light above Dad's head before checking his blood pressure. I leaned over to him and said, "We thought the light might be too bright for you, Dad, but then we remembered that you were blind, so we knew it wouldn't bother you." He wryly commented, "That's true."

It's not that my dad didn't show me love when I was growing up, and it's not as though he was never ornery or moody or frustratingly less than transparent after his stroke. And it's not that we became best friends. But something *did* change within him after his stroke, and that something allowed me to connect with him in ways I had not before.

For all the things Dad gave up, he got something in return. He lost his sight and gained a broader, more all-encompassing vision of life; he lost his spatial orientation and gained the strength to trust others to guide him; he lost his short-term memory and gained the ability to appreciate individual, present moments. This one-man show had transformed into someone who connected gently and honestly with the people around him.

In the last twenty-two years of his life, Dad had to learn to lean on others. He had to learn to be patient and to accept what came his way. But I think he recovered some physical agency in the last month of his life. I think he mustered some of that old Bert Loewen drive and decided it was time for him to go. He chose to stop eating; he chose to stop trying so hard to hear everything we said; he chose to no longer "stay fit for Kae." He chose his time to die. He knew where he was going and he was ready. So he simply lay down and breathed his last. Good on you, Dad!

3. LYNDA

Things my father told me:

"You don't always have to be happy."

So, I was eighteen years old, all the way over in England, attending Capernwray Bible School. I had a return plane ticket dated six months down the road, and I was homesick for the first time in my life. Because it was the first time, I was totally unprepared for it, and things unravelled pretty fast for me.

On one of my phone calls home, as I was explaining how awful I felt, my father said to me, "You don't always have to be happy." This was kind of sharp-edged advice, but I never forgot it. Because it's true. In fact, if you want to be philosophical about it, this is one of the things that all the religious traditions of the world offer their adherents. Not a guarantee that life will be easy, but rather a way to bear suffering. They would say it is our insistence on being happy that keeps us from knowing joy and seeing that there might be a gift in adversity.

Not that I thought all of this when I was eighteen. I was just a young, scared girl, whose father had said it was all right if I was unhappy. That helped a tiny bit. Not as much as a new plane ticket home would have helped, but still.

And when my dad had his stroke and so much was taken from him, I saw him living the truth of what he had said to me: "You don't always have to be happy." Clinging to the ideal life you want will not bring you joy, whereas realizing that you will be miserable a fair amount of your life will help you become less miserable.

⁂

"You're a trooper."

My father was a hobby farmer for a few years. At one point he rented land near Oak Bank, Manitoba, where he enjoyed planting and harvesting in the evenings and on weekends. I remember that it was spring and thus time for seeding. I was sixteen years old and had received my driver's licence the day before. My dad, never one to waste an asset, suggested I drive the truck behind the tractor that he had to transport along the highway. I had driven on the highway exactly zero times. I had driven the truck exactly zero times. However, my father wanted something done, and anyone who knew him will have a sense of how those things usually turned out: they got done.

So, with shaking hands I drove the truck behind his tractor so that he could have a ride home after he dropped it off. I trundled along behind him, trying to keep the right distance back, trying not to care about the traffic speeding by, and not daring to think of what I had to do when the time came to turn off the highway and drive into the field where we would leave the tractor.

Finally, the odyssey was over. He parked the tractor and walked back to where I was waiting by the truck. He put his hand on my shoulder and said, "You're a trooper." It was one of my proudest moments. Dad did not believe in over-praising his children. I basked in the glow of that compliment for a week. And when I think of what my dad gave me that will last, I think it is this capacity to hang in there. What psychologists call "agency." That deep-seated belief that we can make things happen.

And to my father, who lived for twenty-two years blind, dependent, curious, compassionate, undaunted, I say, "You're a trooper, too."

⁂

"Thank you for caring."

We were working at the family homestead in Steinbach: some of my siblings, my mom and dad, my husband, and me. We had been painting and planting and scrubbing, moving in new-old furniture, in preparation for a big family reunion that was happening in just a few days. In the midst of this hustle and bustle, Dad—not untypically—suddenly decided to dig a trench in the yard. He was concerned about the drainage on the property and so got to work on the hard-packed soil, using a spade to create the trough he wanted. My dad was seventy-one years old, rather less sedentary than some men that age, but no gleaming athlete. But we were used to his brainstorms and didn't really give his level of exertion much thought.

We had a bit more furniture to get, and we needed to do it before closing time at the store. My sister and mom and I hopped in the car to drive the few blocks over, but my father wanted to take his bike. Again, we knew better than to question his ideas, so we agreed to meet him there.

Minutes later we were all in front of Solomon's Furniture on Main Street; my father had just parked his bike and we turned to go into the store. But then my father sat down, hard, on the cement steps. A moment later he slumped, head on his chest, listing to one side. He had passed out.

Many things happened after this. Some of us yelled, some of us whispered, some of us tried to get Dad in a suitable position to perform CPR on him while we waited for the ambulance. It occurred to me, belatedly, that if my dad were unconscious, it shouldn't feel like he was resisting me as I tried to move him into a lying-down position to begin resuscitation procedures. Just as my foggy brain was dealing with this confusing development, Dad woke up all the way, looked around and began to talk. So, whatever *had* happened to him, he wasn't about to die.

The ambulance arrived, and all my mother said was that she wished they wouldn't use the siren. We followed behind to the Steinbach hospital. The doctor wanted to take a look at Dad before they let family see him, so it was a while before I was allowed to go into the room where he was resting. He was still pretty out of it, groggy from what turned out to be a fainting spell brought on by his exertion and a faulty heart valve that needed replacing. That subsequent surgery would prove to be a cardiac success, but a neurological failure. Eight months later, as the medical team replaced the defective valve, Dad would have a massive stroke on the operating table. It would take him five weeks to come out of a coma and then two years of rehabilitation to learn to do the most ordinary activities again. It was this stroke that would leave him blind for the last twenty-two years of his life. But neither of us knew anything about that then.

So, I stood above him as he lay on the stretcher. I was crying; relief often makes me cry. And then my dad did something that he had never done before—he reached up, and with his thumb he gently wiped away my tears. And he said, "Thank you for caring."

Well, you're welcome, Dad. You were usually emotionally unavailable, you were very often physically unavailable; as I explained to my own children once, about my upbringing, "I think as soon as my mom and dad got home from their honeymoon my dad went to the door of the house and said over his shoulder as he was leaving, 'See you, Kae—I'll be in a meeting for the next twenty-five years.'"

So, my dad was not always the man I needed him to be. And he knew it. That's why he said what he did. He didn't expect me to care so deeply for him, but he was very touched that I did.

There was a gentleness about my father, and a perceptiveness about him that our often unhappy home obscured. But it existed. He was capable of tenderness. That's probably why I did care.

FINDING MY FATHER

*by **Cari Penner***

I loved my father deeply. I was also fascinated by him. He was hard working, he was handsome, and he held everyone to the same high standard to which he held himself. He never ambled while walking, never hesitated to tackle hard work of any kind, and he played hard, too; whether it was baseball, ping pong, or snowmobiling, he was fearless and determined. I longed to understand what made him the way he was; I wanted to know who he was inside. Ultimately, I did not find what I was searching for. I discovered, instead, something that I had never thought to find: a human being simply trying to be the best husband and father he could be. The following thoughts on my father are my own. Others who knew him well have their own stories, stories that I respect. This is my love story.

I didn't shed a tear at the funeral of my father. He was a stranger to me.

There was no loss of relationship. Years of emotional disconnect had me mourning that disappointment a long time ago. I felt only angry and cheated. I had never really known my father. To me, he was a mystery.

There are many unsolved mysteries in our lives. Mysteries such as who we are and why we exist. Mysteries, too, about why we love and why we do not love, about whom we love and whom we do not love. Mystery draws us in. It begs answers. It wants resolution. So we look for clues—glimpses into lives that matter to us, that may open the door to relationship or, conversely, firmly and conclusively close that same door.

Dad's early years were always mystifying to me. Whenever we children pestered him about his childhood, his answers were cryptic. He hinted at hard times, offered a vague story about having to eat something that he instead threw in the chicken yard, because there was no waste allowed at the table. We got the picture: food was precious in those days. You always ate everything on your plate, and complaints were not tolerated. You were lucky to have any food at all. An avid reader, I was left to imagine scenarios reminiscent of *Oliver Twist*, prairie style, picturing a long table and many hands clawing for scraps of food; dirt and desperation part of the daily diet; patched jackets and hand-me-down shoes. It must have been harsh. There must have been chaos. "I was never a child," he would retort when we asked about his childhood. Our questions were a conversation stopper. But maybe his lack of answers was in fact a clue to his past life.

A child within a family of nine boys and five girls, he had to survive the commotion and lack of attention that a large family living in strained circumstances generated. This inevitable chaos created an enormous drive in him for perfection and control. One of the few photos of my dad as a child shows him nattily dressed in Sunday-best suit and hat, posing with an enormous bicycle. I imagine that bicycle was shared with his fourteen siblings. Finding something to call his own must have been a challenge. Having control over his life and belongings would have been nearly impossible. He must have understood early on that to withstand the chaos of life and eventually become successful, he needed to take control and pursue perfection. This quest began with his clothing and hair and then extended to his manicured lawn and sparkling car. Eventually, he tried to force his children to be perfect, too.

It was as if he wanted to erase any trace of the raucous, desperate life of a large prairie family and morph into a gentleman who never wore scuffed shoes in public.

To all appearances, the Ray Rempel family had it all: a modest three-bedroom home in an established neighbourhood, a thriving downtown business, and upstanding membership at a local Mennonite church. Four children completed the image of a perfect, small-town family.

We certainly looked the part. Our mother, Evangeline, or "Vange," sewed, scrimped, and saved for the requisite dresses, gloves, and matching shoes of the day—her reputation as a well-dressed lady in town was cemented with her attention to detail, her flair for style, and her sense of fashion. We watched in awe as she would appear in Jackie Kennedy–style hats, black patent shoes, or a smart seventies pantsuit. Ray, in particular, proved equal to the pace of changing fashion. The 1950s saw him in a leather jacket, with slicked-back hair. The sixties brought out fitted suit jackets and a brush cut. The seventies were the pinnacle of excess, with his big hair, full moustache, and wide lapels. He kept up a chic appearance for decades, succumbing to track suits and bad T-shirts only when illness finally overpowered his sense of style.

Indeed, his closet was a marvel. I had never seen shirts and jackets hung so carefully; ties of all colours and patterns spun on a special carousel and shoes were lined up in military precision—shoes that were polished religiously on Saturdays, ready to sparkle at church on Sunday morning. In his dresser, belts and socks were organized by colour. I remember snooping in his bedside drawer and finding bits and bobs that told me more about him than he'd ever told me about himself. Still, they were only monogrammed cufflinks, cotton handkerchiefs, and tie pins. There was nothing more than that. The secrets to his real life were kept somewhere else, buried deep. My sister boasted of finding a *Playboy* magazine tucked between the mattress and box spring on his side of the bed. Another clue but also another mystery. Especially intriguing, this one, as my father never mentioned sex to us in any form or fashion.

Except for the time he did.

As Dad got older, he gradually capitulated to various complex methods of hairstyling; he began to allow his hairdresser to use a curling iron on him in an effort to regain his youthful looks. On one occasion, as she attempted to coax his increasingly stiff coif into something fuller, the heat of the iron began to singe his forehead. "Don't burn my foreskin!" he cried. A response

Freud would surely have enjoyed. Dad's face must have turned bright red, and not from the heat of the curling iron. Eventually Vange learned of the incident, and it gradually filtered and spread throughout our family ranks. Because of Dad's reluctance to talk about anything associated with sex, that slip became his children's favourite family story.

I have heard the family unit compared to a mobile, like the kind you see over a baby's crib. Perfectly balanced, it rests easily as long as each part hangs in perfect harmony with the rest. Pull down a piece of the mobile and the whole things shifts wildly off balance, upsetting the delicate weights and wires. Because of my dad's inability to establish close relationships within his family, each member had to try to balance the family mobile in their own fashion.

Mother tried to correct the imbalance through an overabundance of nurturing. Looking back, I see that this response probably only allowed Dad to keep even more emotional distance. In addition to her aggressive nurturing, she also rarely opposed her husband, and then only privately and cautiously. He was the head of the household, after all. While Dad appeared to be the leader of our family, in reality Mom held the reins. Realizing that the emotional tension of family life only highlighted Dad's inability to relate to his children, she became the bedrock of the family, a role she would maintain all her life.

My older sister, Melanie, fought for his attention first with her tomboy phase, becoming the boy she thought he wanted. Soccer, spiders, and mud pies filled her days. The most athletic of all of us, it was easy for her to engage him in throwing a fastball or ice skating, as Dad related to sports and found it easy to interact on that level. As Melanie grew older, Dad's role as gatekeeper was critical as infatuated schoolboys began to knock incessantly on our door to ask her out on dates. She became rebellious in her teen years and never shied from challenging her father on curfews. She would challenge him openly, and the relationship, although assertive and sometimes aggressive on both sides, seemed to matter to both of them. When she became pregnant at eighteen, Dad was distraught by the circumstances and determined to do right by his eldest. She got his attention, surely, as he was forced to acknowledge the realities of her condition; while he acted, he was somehow unable to draw close to her, and after the crisis passed he remained as before, emotionally and relationally inaccessible.

My younger brother's best revenge against his emotionally absent father was to defy every one of Dad's wishes. If Dad wanted him to get a regular job, he proclaimed himself a poet. If Dad wanted him to have a neat and tidy appearance, he dyed his hair bright red, pierced his ear, and wore ripped clothes. Dad wanted him to hold conservative views on everything from politics to potatoes, to find a nice girl, raise a family, and take over the family business. When it became clear that none of this would ever happen, Dad forever abandoned any attempts to foster a father-son bond. Byron spent years away from his family, his community, and his roots, painfully finding his new self, seeing himself as a questing Mennonite Odysseus.

Madrece, the baby, knew my father as the disciplinarian, and a threat to "call Dad"—a phrase used by my mother as a last resort—would bring silent tears to her face. It was one of the few tactics that would evoke that kind of emotion from her. More than ten years have passed since my father's death, and Madrece still responds to the "call Dad" threat. It resonates somewhere deep inside of her. Born with intellectual and physical challenges, Madrece's expectations of my father were eventually limited to being fed, clothed, and housed. She needed love, attention, and care, but he found the role of disciplinarian much easier to fulfill. Emotional connectedness appeared to be beyond his ability, even with a child who would never knowingly thwart his intentions.

As a matter of fact, it was the role of provider and patriarch that my father took very seriously. Like many men of his time, Dad believed order would result when gendered roles were strictly adhered to. Women were meant to cook, clean, have children, and see to warm clothing and washed faces. Men were to be strong, hewers of wood and drawers of water. Thus, my father's sole purpose within his family was to fulfill this role of provider and commanding officer. He took that role seriously, but only that one. It became clear that he could not, or would not, contribute anything else to family life. He gave no fatherly advice on finances, life goals, or relationships. There was no sign of the caring fathers that we saw on *My Three Sons* or *The Brady Bunch*, popular TV shows in my childhood. Of course, those were just fantasies.

As the middle child, I had my work cut out for me when it came to attracting attention from my father. Between Melanie's drama, Byron's defiance, and Madrece's pressing needs for care, there was little space left for me. I was a mild-mannered, eager-to-please young girl, who tried to comply with our parents' every rule, believing that acquiescence would bring the attention I so craved. I tried to be the child who brought order to the chaos within the family. If Dad wanted perfection, then I would be the one to give it to him. In appreciation I'd certainly gain his love and attention as well as the relationship I so desperately wanted. This tactic of acquiescence worked well on my mother. It failed abysmally with my father.

As I grew older and still had not solved the mystery of my father, I found a new heroine to emulate. The *Nancy Drew* book series, about a fictional teen amateur detective, became my new passion. Nancy was strong, independent, and fearless. She and her widowed father were a team, and her successful adventures always gained a nod of approval from her dad. Not surprisingly, I developed an abiding love for these and other mystery stories, and the more subtle and tenuous the clues in the stories the better. The intricate storylines and plots mirrored my own unanswered questions, especially about my father, but in the end Nancy Drew proved more successful with closure than I ever did.

In my teens, I left my innocent childhood behind and turned my unbridled adolescent hormones to boys. I was eager to embrace this new phase of life, to find a partner to share my life with. It was fun at first, but in the end it was disastrous. Desperately looking for that elusive rewarding male relationship, I found that I was wholly unprepared for dating. Time and time again I tried to find a wholesome and honest relationship. Time and time again the relationship would choke and fail. I appeared to be sabotaging my own efforts. Since I had not learned how to connect emotionally with my "mystery" dad, I found I was, in fact, terrified to find what I was so desperately searching for. Would I know how to have a committed, loving, and healthy relationship with a man? I loved my father, but only in the way you can love a person who is untouchable and unknowable. As I sought ways to please him, to reach him, to reveal myself as his daughter, I discovered no sign of reciprocity, no indication that he needed me. I began to question myself, to question my value as a person, my role in life. I, like Byron, began to look for answers. Mysteries always require answers.

Becoming a wife allowed me further insight into the world of men. But the mystery of my father would continue to haunt me, even as I attempted to connect with my husband and sons. I resolved it would be different for me, that there would be closeness and caring between husband and wife. Certainly, marriage was unknown territory, and Dad had given me few lessons on how to achieve matrimonial harmony. It wasn't always easy, but as the years have passed, my husband and I have discovered our own ways of communicating our mutual love and respect. I began to understand that love can be expressed in many ways, with actions as well as with flowery words. Love can be expressed by paying the mortgage, taking out the garbage, or picking up milk on the way home from work. It can reveal itself with a simple hug, a knowing wink, and a shared secret joke. The communication of love is more than what is spoken, and often our actions express our commitment with more conviction than poetry or passionate prose ever could.

As our family grew from two to four, there appeared to be new ways to explore emotional connectedness. I now had the chance to begin afresh, to influence and shape the lives of my two sons in ways I wish had been apparent in my own childhood. And I must have been successful, because Cameron, my oldest, is the polar opposite of my dad, able to access his emotions and connect with me on a personal level that belies my childhood experience. Ryley, our younger child, also has no difficulty expressing love and sentiment in his own way.

As I ponder life with my father, though, it astonishes me to see how much I mirror the enigmatic man who was my dad. This mirroring appears in small things, like how I peel an orange, or how I keep my car clean. Dad could peel an orange so that the peel was one long spiral, perfectly even and unbroken. I can do the same thing with an orange, and do. My own vehicle is washed regularly and is litter free. I keep an ordered, clean home. I have even taken this drive for control and order to the next level by serving on the local city council for many years. Politics is the perfect career for instilling law and order in the land; I have discovered that influencing land use and formulating government policy are ways I can shape my world beyond my home and family. In a way, I have become my father. I realize that I, too, often sacrifice the closeness of relationships at the altar of order and perfection.

Dad was athletic, and I discovered many old trophies from bowling, golf, and baseball competitions in our storage closet at home. These trophies are emblematic of a man who was fiercely competitive. He always soundly beat me at ping pong in our basement. There was no such thing as spotting me extra points; I had to earn my wins on my own. He wanted me to be strong. There was no room for sentiment in these games and, for him, little room for feelings in the game of life.

Dad could fix anything, and his workshop in the basement was a fascination of mine. There was a large white pegboard above the worktable, with each tool's outline in black paint (as if to dare his kids to place the hammer where the saw should be). Byron and I would stare at the workshop, fiddle with forbidden tools, and wonder about this man we knew so little about. We were envious of Melanie, who was able to persuade Dad to build a birdhouse for her school project. The result was a miraculous, beautiful, white cottage with a robin's egg blue roof. It perched proudly on the clothesline Dad had built right outside our dining room window, for all of us to see every day. As an adult, I also now enjoy tackling practical tasks such as small repairs in our home and cottage.

I remember sharing occasional moments with him. In my teens, I began to join him in the early mornings, as he got ready for work. It was just the two of us, me with my makeup and my dad with his razor and shaving cream. I treasured those times, surreptitiously watching him as he patted his face with his bristle brush full of white foam and then carefully scraped it clean. No one else was awake. It was our private moment.

Now and then he would make pork cracklings, a fat-filled, stick-to-your-ribs fry-up that Mom absolutely refused to consider in the early hours of the morning. That and a hunk of white bread and you could last a month in the wilderness.

Sometimes, and this was best of all, he would allow me to miss school and take me to Winnipeg with him when he went to pick up supplies for the business that he and my mother ran. It would be just him and me, all day, with plenty of time between us. I don't understand why he took me, because there appeared to be no special "talks" or reason for our time together, other than the company. And perhaps that was what it was. Company. It made me feel special and confused at the same time. Unanswered questions again.

It was while playing senior baseball that the first hint of Dad's illness appeared. Always quick on his feet, he stumbled as he ran to first base. When the diagnosis of progressive supranuclear palsy was given, it occurred to me that even the name of his illness sounded competitive. A bit of research showed the disease to be an uncommon neurological disease. Nothing ordinary for my dad. As the disease progressed, it manifested itself in his motor skills, his expression, and his balance. All the control and perfection he had built up during his lifetime was falling away. To the delight of his grandchildren, Dad was now the one who giggled during prayer. His curious facial expressions and loud outbursts would irritate my mother during Bible reading at the Christmas gathering, but the kids found him softer and more fun loving that the stern-faced papa he had been before. As adult children, we were completely thrown off balance. This man was not who he used to be. His emotions were unchecked and his body betrayed him. His face began to have the "frozen" look of the disease. But we could not help but hope that in his last years we would find the rewarding relationship that had so eluded us as children. Would this disease open the door to a closer relationship with our dad? Alas, it was not to be. While the illness revealed a more open, less austere man, we could not be sure if what we saw was the true man or merely symptoms of the palsy itself.

Significantly, I simultaneously began to realize that my evaluation of my father was often narrow and immature. He was a product of his generation, as I was of mine. He emerged from a generation that viewed nurture and sentiment as the unique purview of women, and as I came to acknowledge and accept that context, I was able to gradually absolve him of his failures as a father. And once I began to forgive him his shortcomings, I could also embrace my own.

As I thought about his childhood, I slowly began to understand some of the mystery that was my dad. Given his home situation, he likely didn't receive the nurturing he needed as a child. The demands of looking after a large family would surely have been overwhelming for his parents. Certainly, the thirties were not an easy time for anyone. Perhaps the only way he could survive was to find his own "world order"—to go on a quest of his own and create his own path. He did what he could with what he had. And that would have to be enough. I, too, have found my own ways to survive, perhaps even to thrive; I have created my own path as I follow my quest for answers. But I also realize that some answers will never be found.

Parts of my father may have to remain a mystery. There will be some needs that he will never fill. There will be some pieces of his life I will never discover. And I will have to be content with small glimpses into the heart of the first man I ever loved.

TECHNOLOGIES OF AFFECTION

by Ann Hostetler

To write this essay I'm going to have to look at his slides, I tell myself, and so I dig out the projector, untouched at least since his death fifteen years ago. The slides are neatly categorized in labelled boxes, as was his way. But one of my sisters has warned me that the individual slides in each category are randomly mixed; indeed, some of them have fallen out and been carelessly replaced. In his prime my father was a master organizer of his own documentary materials, but at the end, not so much.

When I open the mouldy case, I recognize a scent—something between hair oil and anticipation—associated with family slide shows. My two younger sisters and I would lounge on the sofa or floor, the projector fan humming, the room darkened, and observe the luminous transparencies on the screen, the world through my father's eyes. Alongside his work as a professor and researcher, he was an amateur documentary photographer; every slide he kept held a story. We would beg for these images—"'jecter pictures," we called them—especially in the years before we got our first TV.

My father grew up in an Amish home; Amish children only completed the eighth grade. My father, though, eventually went on to receive a PhD and to write and publish books on the Amish, other plain peoples, and communal groups. Although we lived in a suburb of Philadelphia, it was not so far that we couldn't travel to visit Amish relatives in central Pennsylvania. For my father these visits were special occasions, for which he always wanted my sisters and me to be neatly dressed in modest skirts, our long hair braided.

The only picture of my father as a young child was taken by a visitor who had stopped at the farm in Pennsylvania in 1923; he later sent a print to the family. In this picture, my father, John, is four years old. He stands straight next to his taller brother Jake in front of a rail fence, but unlike Jake, he looks down and away from the photographer.

As a child I scrutinized this black-and-white image of my father—a shy boy in one-suspender overalls, barefoot and peering out from under his dark bangs, eyes squinting into the sunlight—wishing he could turn and look at me so I could see his face.

My father's devotion to photography and documentation contrasts with the Amish prohibition against photographs that he was raised with. He was careful about not violating the consciences of his Amish family and acquaintances, but made sure that his own immediate family was well documented.

I've set up the projector, several cartons of slides at hand, blank wall in front of me, but I can't locate the power cord. After rummaging through the garage, I find one that seems to fit and plug it in. The projector lights up and hums—but it's not the usual hum. Smoke starts rising from the machine. Strange that, although my father didn't last, I assumed his slide projector would outlive him.

I order a replacement—thank goodness for the Internet. Thus begins my own foray into technologies of affection: a projector, a screen, and finally a slide digitizer. Working my way through the slides, I feel close to my father again. Participating in his methods of sorting, organizing, and documenting for posterity is a way of experiencing his world—the things he cared about preserving and his way of framing them.

The first slide I come across is of my father's first wedding, with Hazel Schrock, who died in childbirth two years later along with their child. One slide I'd never seen before shows them gazing at each other with such joy it makes me weep. Then pictures of his second wedding, to my mother, Beulah Stauffer, in Scottdale, Pennsylvania—home of the Mennonite Publishing House, where they met—the two of them walking outside in wedding garb without coats on a warm February Saturday. And then pictures of my father after his PhD graduation, standing next to my mother, Beulah, in front of the empty Penn State football stadium. These are not pictures he took, but pictures he saved. Then I find some he took: a series of my sister Mary and me perched atop a walnut bookcase. We are about four and six.

When Daddy found us on top of the bookcase in our pajamas we expected a scolding, but instead he told us to get dressed so he could take some pictures. We are wearing jumpers and blouses, our hair in braids, our faces absorbed in the books we are reading. I've crossed one leg jauntily over the other, as though I were a teenager.

It occurs to me that family photographs are about being seen. My father more than made up for the photographs not taken of him in his childhood by the pictures he took of us: playing in the sandbox, dressing up in goofy costumes, taking our first bike rides, and doing everyday things. When he worked with the Hutterites, he liked us to dress in the clothes the Hutterites so generously gave us and then take our pictures. (Hutterites don't have the same prohibition against photographs that the Amish do, and, unlike the Amish, they invited us to dress like them.) He took a picture of me with my newly shorn hair at my sixth-grade graduation in a white dress my mother had sewn for me, next to the school's motto from John D. Rockefeller: "What I am to be, I am now becoming." He also took pictures of me with a poison ivy rash all over my face, covered with calamine lotion—my smile revealing the braces I acquired in seventh grade.

His obsession with photography was a hedge against loss. Not only had he missed the opportunity to be photographed as a child; he'd also lost the innocence of his Amish childhood at age eleven when his father was excommunicated and the family moved from Pennsylvania to Iowa in an (unsuccessful) attempt to join an Amish church that did not practice shunning. Later, after he'd left the farm for college, he lost his first wife and first child.

My first five years were spent in Scottdale, where both of my parents were involved with the Mennonite Publishing House. When I was four they agreed to give me an allowance of a quarter a week, which I'd regularly spend on a Little Golden Book at the Provident Bookstore in the publishing house, up the hill from our house. Reading, publishing, and even printing—I visited the press with its linotype machines—were incorporated into my life from the beginning. My father was an author, my mother was an editor and book designer, and they both read to me. But best of all were my father's own stories. He loved to tell about adventures from his Amish boyhood—one in particular in which he and his mother were taking a shortcut to market with the eggs over a railroad bridge when the train came. He was able to help her down onto a trestle and they both escaped with their lives, but just barely. His stories were so vivid that I didn't need pictures to imagine the places and people he described.

During my kindergarten and elementary school years, we lived in five different houses, and I attended four different schools in Canada and the United States. When I turned five my parents moved from Scottdale to Edmonton, Alberta, where my father had been hired as a professor in the sociology department at the University of Alberta. While at the U of A, my father's research focused on the Amish, so every summer we would make the 3,000-plus-mile trip from Alberta to Pennsylvania and back again. When we moved back to Pennsylvania, his research focus became the Hutterites in Canada. Thus, another series of summer trips, to Canada and back again. It seemed normal to me to spend my summers visiting Amish farms and Hutterite colonies. My father's work was, to a degree, our life, and his way of integrating life and work was to get us involved.

I'm in a lecture hall at the University of Alberta with my sister Mary and my parents. Our younger sister, Laura, hasn't yet been born. My father has laid out stacks of papers on seventy-one chairs, and our job is to go from chair to chair, picking up the papers in order and stacking them on a table at the back of the room. We earn a penny for each round completed. We are proud to have such responsibility, and we race each other along the rows, cautious not to miss a page. Afterward, we run outside to play on the perfectly groomed campus grass in our bare feet, thinking this is the most beautiful place on earth, wishing we had a lawn like this at home. Then we ride our bikes with training wheels beside our parents to spend our earnings on ice cream.

We move to Pennsylvania before my third-grade school year, and halfway through the year we move again, from the first house—too small, picked out by my father alone on a trip from Alberta—to one chosen by both my parents that was the right size. We decide to finish the year at our first school, though, which means that we have a twenty-five-minute walk each way. I soon begin to complain of stomachaches on the walk home.

My father tells my sister Mary and me that he'd had the same pains when he was young. "They took my appendix out on the dining room table." We are flabbergasted. "The doctor asked if we wanted to do the operation at home or at his office," he says, "and we thought we might as well have it at home. But I still had the bellyache, even after the operation."

We're sitting on the front porch, and my father reaches into the hedge and picks up a flat, squarish stone with smooth edges. "If you want to cure a bellyache," he says, "look for a stone like this one. A flat one. Then spit on it and throw it over your left shoulder."

"Does it really work?" Mary and I want to know. It certainly sounds better than having your appendix out on the dining room table.

"Why don't you try it and see?" he suggests, a slight grin on his face. Sure enough, on a hot afternoon a few days later, my side begins to ache fiercely. I find a flat, squarish stone at the edge of the sidewalk and pick it up, spit on it, and throw it over my left shoulder. Almost immediately my stomachache disappears.

"Let me try," Mary exclaims.

"Do you have a side-ache?" I am skeptical. She just wants to copy me.

"A little one."

She picks out a stone and spits on it, throws it over her shoulder. "My tummy ache is all gone," she says, jumping up and down. We are so excited that we run all the way home, racing each other to be the first one to tell Daddy how well his cure worked.

We ask him for more of his mother's remedies. He tells us that she knew how to cure a colicky baby by passing it around a table leg three times and chanting a rhyme. Our little sister Laura is a colicky baby, but she's way too wiggly to pass around a table leg. We ask him to teach us the rhyme. "Maybe someday," he says, but I sense his reserve. Someday he might pass it on to one of us, he says, as his mother had passed it on to him, but the transmission of powwowing is not something to be shared casually. We each secretly long to be chosen.

A few years after our move back to Pennsylvania, I'm visiting an antique and "junk" store with my father. We've wandered into the back rooms full of furniture, framed pictures, dishes, knickknacks. I stop by a little desk, just my size—I'm over five feet now, a sixth-grader. "It's an old sewing table," my father explains. It looks just right for me: three drawers on the side, a foldout wooden table for a top. He finds a chair that fits, and I have a "new" desk. After we bring it home, he cleans it up and refinishes it for me. It fits perfectly into my bedroom, and I use its drawers to hold my stationery and sealing wax, its surface to write my first poems.

I'm sitting beside my father in the audience at the Amish Farm and House, one of Lancaster County's oldest tourist venues. The guide tells us that the Amish paint their walls and buy window shades only in blue and green, because those are the colours of the grass and sky. Is that really why Aunt Lizzie, my father's oldest sibling, who is still Old Order Amish, has dark green blinds at her windows? I listen, entranced that the colours of nature are so honoured in Amish life, but I'm also skeptical that the non-Amish guide is making it all up. Afterward, I ask my father whether the guide is right.

"Never heard of it!" he said. I asked whether we should set the tour guide straight. My father declines. "It's just our job to listen in."

I'm sitting beside my father at his desk, a big one of dark polished wood, seasoned with use—a discard from the Mennonite Publishing House—which he used for his entire adult life. It has two wooden leaves, one on either side of the pencil drawer, and he's pulled out one for me to use as my own writing desk. We're collaborating on a story based on the Hostetler massacre, the one chronicled in *The Descendants of Jacob and Barbara Hochstetler*, which we've read together over and over.

"Why didn't they use their gun, Daddy?"

"The gun was only for hunting. The Bible teaches that 'thou shalt not kill.'"

"Not even when your own family is being attacked?"

The mother, the daughter, and the son with the broken leg were killed. The father and his other two sons were taken captive. I figured I wouldn't have stood much of a chance of survival in a similar situation. The story dramatized the classic dilemma posed to nonresistant Christians: *If you would kill to save your family, why would you not join the army and kill to save your country?*

"But wouldn't Jacob have at least tried to save his wife?"

The wife was stabbed through the heart by the Indians—a dishonourable death—ostensibly because she had refused them bread when they had come to her door earlier. I learned to bake bread in high school, taught my friends to bake, and shared the bread. It wasn't until decades later that a friend helped me interrogate this story about an ungenerous woman. "Perhaps the woman was terrified to open the door," she suggested. "Perhaps she didn't have enough food for her own children."

Although the story provided no desirable female role models, I paid attention to the sons' and father's intriguing adventures and escape stories. I attempted illustrations. But my drawings disappointed me; I never finished the project. Now I realize that the project provided a framework—a technology of the word, if you will—for my father and me to share and interact with a text that demonstrated the larger narratives of our ancestors and our faith. I'm still wrestling with those narratives that have been culturally encoded through time.

My father purchased a copy of *Martyrs Mirror* for each of his daughters—two Ephrata *Martyr's Mirror*s and an illustrated *Martyr's Mirror* from Holland, with the Jan Luyken illustrations. He was also a collector of Amish and Hutterite bonnets, hats, and head coverings. These I longed to try on, along with the nurse's cape that was a legacy from Hazel, his first wife. However, I was rarely allowed to do so. These were not dress-ups; they were heirlooms. Only once were we allowed to try them on—while posing for a photograph.

In addition to taking pictures, my father recorded Amish singing and interviews. (The Amish prohibition against technology did not seem to apply to the tape recorder.) Of course, he also practised this technological documentation on his family. When we were in grade school, it was fun to hear the recordings my father sometimes made of us, though we squealed when we heard our own voices because they sounded so funny to us. When I was an adolescent, however, his tape recorder was much less welcome in my life.

My father probably thought I was enjoying myself, tangled up in the extra-long phone cord on the floor between the kitchen (where the phone was) and the dining room (where the carpet was), talking to my friends. But secretly, I dreaded long phone calls with friends who were seeking to pass the time and the pressure of having to come up with something to say. Being somewhat on the "participant observer" fence at the prep school I began attending in seventh grade, I didn't know how to politely excuse myself and still keep my friends. When my father tells me that he has recorded one of these conversations, I'm furious. I'm already trying so hard to be accepted in school—the last thing I need is to be subjected to the gaze of the amused "father-anthropologist."

During my teens, my father started taking me with him on his evening walks after supper, and this proved to be a great blessing. Instead of his tape recorder, I had his ears, his companionable silence, and access to his creative side. I did most of the talking. He did most of the listening. We were philosophers of the universe, and everything was up for reinvention. The night felt limitless and open outside the orderly house with its routines and regimens and duties.

When I turned sixteen, the family went to live in Vienna, Austria, for a year. My father wanted to spend his sabbatical studying the origins of the Hutterites in Moravia. My sisters and I had wanted to go to Austria since we'd seen *The Sound of Music*, the first movie we ever saw as a family. I've since discovered that this landmark was shared by many Mennonite families of my generation—hardly a surprise considering it's a family-oriented film about anti-Nazi German-speakers that also features singing in four-part harmony. When my sisters and I saw the film, we begged to go to

Austria, and when a few years later we did, we thought the whole trip had been our idea.

During the year in Vienna, we all came to know one another better, living together in a two-bedroom flat. I was impressed with my mother's improvisational skills: making a three-course meal with only one kettle when we first arrived; shopping for fabric and renting a sewing machine that required an impressive mechanical know-how; and teaching me how to make yeast bread from the whole-grain flours I hunted down in health food stores. My sister Mary studied violin with members of the Vienna Philharmonic, and my youngest sister, Laura, studied for several hours each day, coping with third-grade assignments that included crocheting and doing arithmetic with a fountain pen. My father and I continued our evening walks, at least for the first part of the year, peering into the closed shop windows and dreaming about life. He also took a lot of naps. He was writing.

Because I was attending a Gymnasium and knew little German, my task was to listen in. I became, in effect, a participant observer. Having little homework and lots of time on my hands, I began using my father's camera. This was the era in which film and developing were expensive—long before everyone had a camera phone with immediate digital feedback. I loved framing and photographing everything that captured my interest, from springtime blossoms to my youngest sister (eight years younger) playing in nearby Türkenschanz Park. In fact, when we were on a sightseeing trip, my father would often hand me the camera and allow me to take the pictures. He saved them all in a blue case.

In Vienna, I fell in with a group of American teenagers—mostly diplomats' children—who had been evangelized by a charismatic missionary from Indiana who had brought them the gift of tongues. This was the era of George Harrison's "My Sweet Lord" and Jesus freaks. I met an attractive long-haired guy a few years older than me, and he invited me for a ride on his moped to a play at the American school. My father was not in favour of this, which meant that he became silent and ground his teeth, while my mother interpreted for him.

My crush on the moped driver did not develop, but I did attend revival meetings at his parents' swank apartment (kids only) and became convinced that, unless they were on fire for the Lord, our parents' faith was in serious need of renewal. I remember one evening returning home to my sedate parents and asking them about this. They gave me a copy of J.B. Phillips's translation of the New Testament in Modern English and encouraged me to read it myself. I slept on the foldout living-room couch that year, next to my parents' bedroom, reading into the night, writing in my journal, musing about life. One morning I awoke from a pleasant dream, in which God, from a distance, was mightily amused and I was fine.

After they married, my parents went to Germany. My father had a Fulbright scholarship at the University of Heidelberg and my mother was copyediting *The Complete Works of Menno Simons* for Herald Press. They came home early when the later stages of her pregnancy with me became wearing. Perhaps the family trip to Vienna was a bit like a second honeymoon for them, this time with kids and more resources. My mother, who had started graduate school in Religious Thought at the University of Pennsylvania the year before, had a project, too. She used the year in Vienna to study for her language exams while caring for us so my father could write. We travelled extensively—even to countries in the Eastern Block: Czechoslovakia and Hungary—where my father was doing the bulk of his research. He took the trip to Romania alone, however, and came back a few days late with a new tale of harrowing escape, when his visa had blown out the window of our VW microbus in "no man's land" and he had tried to get out of the car and retrieve it while the guards were waving their guns at him. After having to turn around on a Friday evening and spend more than a little extra time in Romania, he had managed to find a connection that could pull him through.

My father's interest in American politics influenced his daughters toward civic-mindedness. His political interests first surfaced in my consciousness when we were living in Alberta in 1959 and 1960: he ardently followed the Kennedy election on the radio and painted an enthusiastic verbal portrait of this young candidate. Even though I was only six years old, I heard the hope and enthusiasm in his voice. In 1962 we moved to the United States, and a year later, when I was nine, I was devastated by Kennedy's assassination. We watched the funeral on the neighbour's TV and the following year bought our first television, a small black-and-white portable.

Six years later I watched the Democratic National Convention on TV with my parents, fuming at the neglect of Robert's Rules of Order and the railroading through of Hubert Humphrey's nomination. My parents had allowed me to canvass for Eugene McCarthy that summer (I was thirteen turning fourteen), and I took the convention hard, especially when Mayor Daley's police in their riot helmets were photographed attacking protesters in Chicago. This was also the year of the Prague Spring, and I couldn't help but make comparisons. A few years later when we went to Vienna, we travelled to Prague and saw the bullet holes made in the public buildings by Soviet tanks.

My parents subscribed to *Life, Look, The Saturday Review*, and *Newsweek* alongside the Mennonite periodicals—*Mennonite Weekly Review, Christian Living*, the *Gospel Herald*. My father also subscribed to the Amish newspaper *The Budget* and other periodicals from Pathway Publishing, including *Family Life* and *The Blackboard Bulletin*. The Sunday *New York Times* also brought the world into our home. This wide variety of reading material created a unique synthesis of worldly news, Mennonite critique, and Amish piousness. As I grew older, one of my father's most frequent conversation starters was sharing an article with me and asking for my feedback. He eventually began to ask me to edit his writing. I didn't realize then that I'd taken up a role vacated by my mother when she started graduate school.

My father wrote in drafts. He was intuitive with language; he began with a gestalt he wanted to get across in the linear medium of writing. He started with an image or an impression and then hammered it out in words. Long before Anne Lamott came out with her famous *Bird by Bird* book on writing, with its chapter "Shitty First Drafts," he used the method she describes, starting out humbly with a draft and improving remarkably with each revision, building up the surfaces of his typescripts: frescoed layers of pencil, correction fluid, cut and paste. The final product had a sense of voice and thoughtful authority. The reader saw the world through my father's layered lens. I was never responsible for the essence of what he conveyed—my help was merely that of a careful reader. But I did provide an audience and companionship, and perhaps drawing on my editorial skills was his way of staying connected with me, including me in his often solitary work.

After college, my parents encouraged me to attend the University of Denver Publishing Institute in its first year. I discovered my own passion for publishing and editing through this six-week summer program and ended up in New York City, staying with a friend my parents had met through my father's work on the Amish. After working for several years, first at Doubleday in the publicity department and then at George Braziller as the promotions manager, I loved my work but was less than satisfied with the New York singles scene. I mentioned to my parents one weekend that perhaps arranged marriages weren't so bad if your parents knew you well and had your happiness at heart. A few months later, when I came home to Philadelphia for the weekend, I was introduced to a young man working on a study of Amish school children. After his visit, my father sent me the young man's resume. Pretty soon the young man showed up in New York on a "business trip," and we hit it off so well that we are still together forty years later.

We spent the summer of 1983 with my father in Alberta and British Columbia on one of his last major trips, researching a communal group that called itself "The Body of Christ." He'd discovered this group through the Hutterites, who felt sorry for the ill-equipped Americans living on the land near their own highly developed communal farms and preparing for the "end times."

I was pregnant with our first child, the perfect excuse to duck out when "just listening" became too much for me to bear. We stayed with families in their lean-to dwellings and walked through the mud in rubber boots to meals and worship services in the common house, where the newly liberated Christians would sing and "speak in tongues." We drank water from their rain barrels, used their bucket toilets and outhouses, stayed in the curtain-partitioned bedrooms they shared with us. Every few days my father knew we needed a break, so he'd suggest we take a research time-out in Dawson Creek or another nearby city, to stay in a hotel and eat in restaurants while we processed our immersion.

The birth of his first grandchild, Elizabeth, whom I carried during that summer research, deepened my connection to my father, for whom birth had been a traumatic as well as a miraculous experience. Elizabeth was breech, and my doctor insisted on a C-section because this was a first delivery for me. I think this was a relief for my father; he repeatedly told me that a C-section would have saved the lives of his first wife and child. I owe my existence to his willingness to try marriage and family a second time.

As his daughters grew into adults, married, and had families, "Opa," as we began to call him when Elizabeth was born, made regular short visits to our homes, offering to help with child care or minor household repairs. My parents, in their later years, enjoyed hosting family dinners on Sundays, fostering conversation among the newer members of the family, their children, and their guests.

In 1993 Elizabethtown College held a conference on the Amish, which included a thirtieth-anniversary celebration of my father's book *Amish Society*, just released in its fourth edition. The entire family gathered to support him, and during the evening he introduced me to Julia Spicher Kasdorf, the poet and scholar. She read from her research on J.W. Yoder, the first writer of note from Kishacoquillas ("Big") Valley—a valley that Julia shared in common with Yoder and my father. In *Sleeping Preacher*, her award-winning first book of poems, she gave life to our shared valley in art and led me to the work I now do as a scholar and poet and collector of poetry and literature by Mennonite writers, helping me integrate these vocations with my own Amish and Mennonite roots. My father's introduction demonstrates his alertness to making connections for others—and his investment in the next generation.

As my father began to age, the early signs of dementia appeared. After a mild heart attack at age seventy-five, he was diagnosed with depression and anxiety. He had panic attacks that would send him to the emergency room. After he visited four times in one week, the nurses instructed him to go home and call in the morning. I visited as often as I could.

I'm sitting cross-legged on the Berber wool carpet in the living room in Willow Grove, Pennsylvania, next to the round coffee table, my father beside me on the sofa.

"I can't remember what it's called, this thing I have," he tells me. "But it starts with a *D*."

"Depression?" I ask. He nods, a bit shame-faced. Mental illness was not discussed, except occasionally in relation to severely encumbered relatives.

I open *The Language of Life*, a book I've brought him. It's a series of interviews that Bill Moyers conducted with poets. I read to him from the section on Jane Kenyon, who wrote about displacement, and loss, and her depression. The elegant simplicity of the poems, their rural subjects and devotional tone, soothe him for the time being.

I stay overnight in my childhood bedroom and wake to see my father at the door in his bathrobe. "I think we need to go to the hospital," he says. This is the first panic attack of his I've experienced. His body is tensed and rigid, his eyes fearful, his presence urgent.

"Just breathe deeply," I tell him. "Make sure that you breathe out as long as you breathe in." I walk him down to the living room where he sits in a reclining chair, lulling himself back to sleep as I coach his breathing.

The next day I show him how to do simple exercises to relax his shoulders. He stands opposite me in the living room, attempting to mimic shoulder rolls. All he can manage is a stiff up-and-down movement. I make a mental note: develop a physical practice of movement so that when old age sets in, I'll still have body memory.

We sit back down and I start to read to him from Thich Nhat Hanh's *Peace Is Every Step*. My father's old age has brought me the insight that the present is all we truly have. Being in each other's presence is the greatest gift.

⁂

We're seated around the dining room table at my parents' new home in Goshen, Indiana, within walking distance of church, campus, and hospital. My mother, eight years younger than my father, has just recovered from quadruple bypass surgery, and with our encouragement my parents have moved from their home in Pennsylvania to the city of their alma mater. Here they are closer to two of their daughters, who have relocated to the Midwest. There is an Amish community close by for my father to visit, intellectual stimulation for my mother, friends for both of them, my sister Laura's in-laws next door. We've worn a path from Wisconsin to Indiana to supervise the renovation of the house we've helped them pick out. Now the newly refinished floors gleam underneath the familiar walnut dining table. My mother serves roast chicken bought from a local farmer. The next year, I accept a job in Goshen College's English department. We move, with our four children, to a house on the same street as my parents and start a new adventure, part of which is staying present with my parents in their final years.

My father died in August 2001, two weeks before the towers fell in New York City. In the last months he sensed such turbulence in the world that he seems clairvoyant in retrospect. My father's visitation was in the College Mennonite Church Chapel down the hall from the room in which I was teaching a class on Native American literature. I started a film for my students, walked to my father's viewing, and afterward returned to class. Community is a great comfort in a time of world turbulence. My office at Goshen College is on a corner surrounded by hospital, church, funeral home, and the former house of Harold and Elizabeth Bender, Goshen College legends—a place I visited with my parents when I was a child. It is a hub of birth, marriage, transition, and death—intertwined with memories of life and death, education, and discovery and becoming.

The week after my father's death, I clean out the makeshift study my father had set up in the basement. He has just a few filing cabinets here, along with his old wooden desk from the publishing company; he's given the rest of his papers to the Pennsylvania State University library. In a file drawer I find a meagre assortment of folders, including one labelled "Resume of things I said No to." I laugh out loud at his dry humour. Even after his death he is gently advising me. A warm feeling of love made palpable steals over me. His desk, his empty file drawers, his worn address book—all are husks of a great loving spirit released from material form. I am filled with awe at the love he invested in me over the years. His spirit of curiosity, faith, and joy carry on in me. I write with gratitude for this gift, his faith in my becoming.

SEVEN TIMES WITH MY FATHER

*by **Magdalene Redekop***

one: the time I talked back to my father with impunity

It was a Sunday afternoon. We had church visitors at the farm and all of us were gathered in the *groute schtove* (the large common room). Somebody asked me what I planned to be when I grew up. Before I could answer, my father said, in Low German, "Magdalene is going to be a doctor." If you know anything at all about what Mennonite fathers expected from their daughters in rural Manitoba during the 1950s, then you might assume that I thanked him. Perhaps Shakespeare was right about the thanklessness of a child being sharper than a serpent's tooth. I knew that my father had dreamt of being a doctor himself and that he was in awe of his good friend Dr. Cornelius Wiebe, who had delivered me and thousands of other babies. I also knew that my father often consulted a big green book called *Kehrt zur Natur Zurück* (Go back to nature) for advice on how to deal with various health emergencies. (If you step on a rusty nail, for example, pull up some camomile plants from the ditch, put them in a basin of hot water, and soak your foot.) Because I thought I knew that my father was projecting his personal dream onto me, I informed our visitors that I was going to decide for myself what I would be when I grew up. I vaguely remember shocked looks on the faces around me. On my father's face there must have been hurt, and I am now sorry I caused it. But what I mostly remember is that he did not reproach me and that, if anything, he looked proud. As if to say to his guests, See what I mean? This kind of indulgence may be what led me to go too far another day.

two: the time I talked back to my father and my world came to an end

It was my first year at Altona Collegiate Institute, and going to school in town meant that my father had to interrupt his farm duties every day to drive my sister and me to and from school. On this particular day I had been given a detention by the German teacher because my friend Gloria and I had laughed in class. It happened while he had his back turned and was writing a list of German words on the blackboard. We noticed that he had capitalized words that should not be capitalized, and that he had done so because he had taken them out of our textbook, where those particular words were at the beginnings of sentences. When he turned around and caught us giggling he demanded to know why. I pointed out which of the words listed should not be capitalized unless they were the first word in a sentence. His petulant response was, "But I took them from the beginning of a sentence!" Of course this made us laugh even harder and triggered an inexorable chain of events: me being served with a fifteen-minute detention; me coming out of school late; me getting into the back seat of the car, where my father and older sister had been waiting; me being subjected to a scolding while my father began to drive home.

What I remember from that scolding is that my father said, "*Ekj schame me zou.*" I am so ashamed. To which I responded, from the back seat, "*Na dann schamt jünt mol.*" Go ahead! Be ashamed then! That's how an English version of the exchange would sound today. In Low German my insult was cushioned just a little bit because my use of the word "*jünt*" meant that I was saying, "Well then shame thyself once." None of us ever addressed our parents as *Dü* (the informal word for "you") but there was a sense in which *Papü*, which is what we usually called our father, was like a term of endearment—not a formal word like *Foda*.

It was my *Foda* who responded when I said those words. He slammed on the brakes and the car stopped with a lurch. We were right in the middle of an intersection in downtown Altona, at the centre of two crossing streets. I don't remember any traffic at all, school having been out for some time. I do remember the feeling in the pit of my stomach, which was how you feel if you think of time as a flat road and realize you have come to the very end of that road.

But life goes on. Later that day, after a strained *Ovenkust* (supper) during which my siblings gave me pitying looks, my parents spoke in hushed tones behind their bedroom door. When they emerged, my father went straight to the barn to finish the chores, and my mother told me that I must write a letter of apology to the teacher. That was so hard to do that I did not even think about something that strikes me now, for the very first time, as remarkable: never once did my father insist that I apologize to him for "talking back."

three: the time my father called me Schveetheart

When it comes to large Mennonite families, once the baby in the family, always the baby in the family. My eleven older brothers and sisters took turns telling me that I was the only one in the family that had a second name—that my father called me Magdalena Schveetheart Fauljk. When he said the word "sweetheart" he always did it with a deliberate accent to make sure nobody would suspect he knew any English. That bit about me being the only one—I eventually came to see that as a family myth. I now believe that my father used similar endearments for his other children when they were very young. But because I was the youngest, I enjoyed a prolonged time of physical affection from my parents. This was especially apparent with relation to something we called *uppe schout zette*—sitting on the lap. There are pictures of me sitting on my mother's lap when I was already school age. I cannot quite remember sitting on my father's lap, but I do almost remember a time when he called me Schveetheart. To be more precise, I have just the faintest trace of a physical memory: a warm glow on my cheek from my father rubbing it with his cheek. My computer tells me it is called stubble burn, but stubble was what my father burned out on the fields.

It may be that I cherish the memory of that spot of warmth on my cheek because it was the last time I ever touched my father, unless you count the day of my wedding when the photographer instructed me to pretend to adjust the flower on the lapel of my father's jacket. I remember thinking, as I did that, how surprisingly easy it was to do and how much I loved him. That it was no big deal was significant given our family history. I had a maternal grandfather who touched little girls in the wrong places. He never touched me, but as I grew older and saw the enormity of the damage done by my grandfather, I was always grateful for the respectful physical distance of my father's love. I was also relieved that my father never spanked me—all the more so after witnessing the terrifying sound of my older sister being beaten behind the closed door of our tiny washroom while she screamed "*Ekj vou bede.*" I will pray.

Maybe I was my father's favourite and maybe not, but I was always conscious of my great good fortune in being the youngest child. By the time I was born our *Papü* was mellowing—a lovely word that always makes me think of autumn leaves—and by the time I left home he had retired. As Ältester Wilhelm Falk, he had been in some ways a remote figure, almost a stranger to me. Later in life when I heard their stories about him, I came to wonder if perhaps he had been more physically demonstrative with my older brothers and sisters when they were little, before the church claimed him so completely.

When I told a friend, whose father is Greek, that I was never hugged by my father once I became an adult, she was shocked and wondered how I had survived. It had to be enough for me, and it was. In fact, after years of teaching, I developed a theory (based on my impressions from talking to students) that for a woman to be successful in the public sphere, the most important factor is a father who believes in her. It was enough for me that he did that. You can have a father who is remote as long as you never doubt that he loves you. On the other hand, I have to admit that it was also not enough. I still remember the last time I saw him, how I longed to hug him and did not dare. That I did not remains one of the deepest and most lasting regrets in my life.

four: the time my father embarrassed me and I hated him for it

These times with my father are like beads on a string, and they come in different colours. This one is black. It was a moment that was embarrassing on more levels than I can count. It happened because I was slow to learn to play the piano by ear. My older sisters had all managed this at an early age. In later years I would tease my sister Martha that she was born arms first, reaching for a keyboard. My mother often told the story of how Martha was only four when she sat down at the piano and played and sang: "O happy day! O happy day! When Jesus washed my sins away!" Not only did I never get saved in that dramatic way, but (and for me this was worse) I also could not play the piano and sing about that event.

Seeing that I needed help to get started, my mother dug into the precious family allowance cheque to pay for piano lessons for me. I was in grade seven and Mrs. Hildebrandt, the teacher at our one-room school, had offered to teach piano after school in her house on the grounds of Roseville School. On this particular day I was sitting on the piano bench next to Mrs. Hildebrandt as she turned the page to the piece I had been practising that week. It was some kind of minuet—not exactly "O Happy Day," but still a pretty tune. After she turned the page Mrs. Hildebrandt and I sat in silent shock for a while. At the top of the page there was a line drawing of people dancing. Except that you could no longer see them. They were slashed out with angry black crayoning.

After a while Mrs. Hildebrandt said something like "What happened here?" I still marvel at how quickly I came up with a lie: I told her that one of my nephews must have gotten hold of the book. I never found out whether she actually believed me or whether she just pretended to in order to spare me embarrassment. The teachers at Roseville School were certainly aware of my father's strict rules for his daughters on matters to do with dress and hair that might lead to dancing. When all the other children went on a Valentine's Day outing to Altona to the skating rink, my father's fear of dancing meant that I alone stayed behind in the empty school. When they all returned with rosy cheeks and happy chatter, I pretended that I had enjoyed my time alone to read. Possibly I fooled my classmates, but I doubt that I fooled the teacher.

Now that I am a parent myself I can imagine how worried my father must have been for the future of the daughter who dared to talk back to him. On that day there was no opportunity to talk back, but I had a mental picture of him bent over my music book with black crayon in hand. It stirred in me an anger that burned like a flame, a searing anger that felt like hatred and that made me want to get as far away from my *Foda* as I possibly could.

five: the time I made my father smile

Colour this one red and sprinkle it with white polka dots. It happened while I was sitting at the dining room table with my parents. I was visiting from Toronto. They had moved to Plum Coulee after my father retired from farming, to a bungalow that had luxuries like a flush toilet and an automatic dishwasher. By this time I was a doctor, although not the kind that my father had in mind when he made his prediction. Despite the unaccustomed luxuries and free time, my parents were lonely and my father was suffering from depression. I tried to think of how I could let him know how much I loved and respected him, how grateful I was to him for all he had given me.

Recently I had been thinking about why we reread some books and not others, and remembering how often I had reread *Jean Val Jean* during my years in Roseville School. There were not many books on the school shelves and I was a voracious reader, so if I wanted to read, I had to read a book more than once. There were only so many times you could reread *The Robe*, but *Jean Val Jean* (as told by Solomon Cleaver) was shorter and the book even contained photographs. It was a popular digest version of Victor Hugo's *Les Miserables* written by a young preacher in Winnipeg and illustrated with fourteen scenes from a French film version of the novel.

The kind-hearted bishop in *Jean Val Jean* who offers hospitality to Jean did not look at all like my father. His hair was too long and he was wearing a strange costume. That did not stop me, as a child, from conflating the two bishops. After all, when people spoke English my father was addressed as Bishop Falk. The pictures in that book always made me think of how my father responded when "the Indians" came to Bishop Falk's house to "beg." Such words are considered offensive now, but they were the ones used by everybody in our community at the time. My father did not seem to think of these people as beggars. He would invite them to sleep in the *Scheen*, the hay barn, and we would provide them with food and blankets. In the morning he would let them fill their truck with gasoline from our big tank before they left. It may be that there were other farmers who responded with kindness, but I did not know of any. Very likely my father's kindness was an expression of guilt, although he would not have had the clear sense we now have of the dispossession suffered by Indigenous people. What I did know was that my father's way of interacting with them did not fit with how "Indians" were spoken of in our community at the time. I was proud of him. As I pondered these things during my flight from Toronto to Winnipeg, I found myself remembering, in particular, one elderly man who was accompanied by his grandson. My father seemed to have a special bond with him. At least once he let them sleep in his *shtäfche*, the tiny room on the second floor where he prepared his sermons.

When I arrived in Plum Coulee I discovered that my father's memory was failing, likely because of his long struggle with depression. I felt an urgent desire to help him remember this specific instance of his kindness and hospitality. Hoping to provide a memory hook, I told him that this particular old man had always used a colourful handkerchief. When I tried to describe it, however, I came up against the language barrier. "*Rout*" is the Low German word for red. But how do you say "polka dots" in Low German? Even my mother did not know. She was a woman who laughed easily and often, and now she began to show signs that she was trying to hold in her laughter for fear of hurting my feelings. My father never laughed and seldom smiled, but now he was looking at me with a smile on his face. I was too obsessed with the polka dots to pay attention, but my father's rare smile finally emboldened my mother to tell me that I was making a mistake. She reminded me that we did not talk *prust* (crude) at home. Why did I keep talking about a "*Schnuddadök*" when the right word is "*Schneppeldök*"? I don't know the meaning of *schneppel*. Maybe to snuffle or sniff. The literal translation of *Schnuddadök* is snot rag.

six: the time I overheard my father speak English

It happened, late in his life, when my father was being treated for depression after the death of his twin brother, Derk. This was the brother who, during the very years that my father was Ältester of the *Rudnerweider Kirchengemeinde*, distinguished himself as the town bum in Altona. I know it sounds like another tale by Victor Hugo—the bishop and his twin brother, the drunkard—but the story is more complicated than that. My father's oldest brother, Henry, had shot himself in 1939; not long after that, all my father's siblings, with the exception of his twin brother and one sister, had moved to the United States, where they assimilated into mainstream English-speaking culture. They were hardly ever spoken of in our family, and this happened before I was born. It was many years before I began to wonder whether these vanishings were a response to the shame of Henry's suicide. Eventually, somewhere down in the States, my father's brother David and two of David's sons also committed suicide. So when my Uncle Derk finally succumbed to the slower suicide of alcoholism, it is small wonder that my father was hit hard.

When I was a teenager I did not fully appreciate that my father's choice— to stay in Manitoba and accept the leadership role that was thrust upon him—made him an anomaly in his own family. What was more important for me at that age was that he stubbornly refused to speak English. We children were allowed to speak English to one another but with him we could speak only Low German, a language he feared would not survive. His beloved mother had died too soon, and when he spoke of his *mutta sprök* it almost seemed as if he was trying desperately to keep his mother's spirit alive. The few times he could not get out of speaking English—for example, during a rare visit from one of his American brothers—he would make fun of himself, exaggerating his Low German accent and speaking in ridiculous chopped up fragments. When I married one of those *Russländer* who had not learned to speak Low German, communication got even harder. On one of my visits home I lost my voice completely because of the strain of inadequate translation between my husband and my father. So you can see why my jaw dropped when I overheard my father speaking fluent English. It happened during one of my visits from Toronto. He had just been released from the hospital, and I was relieved to find that he was recovering. I knew that he had been at the point where he could not get out of bed or shave or eat, but with the help of medication he was now once again at home in Plum Coulee. On the day of his checkup—a doctor's appointment at the Eden Mental Health Centre—my mother suggested I drive to Winkler in her little blue Datsun to pick him up. I was a little early, so I sat down on a bench in the hallway outside the office just as my father and his doctor emerged.

The conversation had something to do with the weather—nothing really important. What shocked me was that my father was conversing in English just like anyone else might do, with barely a trace of a Low German accent.

seven: the time my father taught me that the earth is round

I learned many things from my father that have served me well all my life, lessons that mostly cannot be put into words. Perhaps most important is that he taught me, by example, that the only way to keep living at all, the only way to move forward, is to accept the contradictions in myself. One of these contradictions is that I can both love and hate the same person. Ambivalence tends to be most intense in the relationship between a parent and a child, precisely where in our culture it is most fervently smeared over with sentimentality.

My father definitely thought he was teaching us how to get to heaven and avoid going to hell, but the lesson that stuck with me was that death is part of life. This seventh time with my father is not one time but many times. Not the kind of times that can be laid out in a chart, like the times table, but more like how time is on a farm. Ours was only slightly above a subsistence farm, but we did not know that we were poor. There was always enough to eat and we knew exactly where our food came from. The sun always rose and set in the same place in that big sky, and although the winters were long and hard, spring always came and with it seedtime and then harvest. The kind of time that my father preached about in church, the kind that could suddenly be interrupted with a Second Coming or come to an end like one of those two flat roads—the straight and narrow going to heaven or the winding one going to hell: the kind of time that was frightening. It did not fit with how we lived. What was real and what you could smell and see and touch was how time went round and round. When we celebrated Christmas and Easter, then cyclical time intersected with church time in a way that was deeply comforting because it fit with life on the farm as I knew it.

It was to be many years before I would come to realize that my difficulty with the study of history had to do with being Mennonite, with how we have sought to define ourselves as living outside history altogether. At the time I just knew that the dates in my textbooks meant nothing to me at all, and that rote memorization of them was agony. Geography was a problem, too. Unlike history, it was right there outside the windows of Roseville School. I could smell it and see it, but the map on the wall was another story. It was something you could unroll so that it covered the blackboard but it was at the wrong end of the schoolroom. If I imagined it laid out flat, then the north of the map was pointing to Altona, which was actually south. This confused me so utterly that I never got over it. To this day, when I travel to various cities in the world and look at a map, I have to imagine myself in Roseville School and perform a mental flip of north and south so as not to get lost. There were those in our community who thought the earth was flat. My father was not one of those, although he did insist that the Russians were lying about Sputnik.

Which brings me to that moment in time when my father taught me that the earth is round. We were on our way back from Altona in the '53 forest green Ford, just me and my father. I used to join him when he drove to town to do the shopping and to run church errands. He would buy me a bag of jelly beans to enjoy on the way home. On this particular day he stopped at the roadside to check on one of his fields. He would often do that, savouring the beauty of the waving fields of grain and sometimes walking out into the field to pull up an unsightly wild mustard weed. On this day he walked out into the field until I could not see him at all, leaving me sitting in the car with my bag of jelly beans. I was in a quandary. If I ate them all, I would feel selfish. If I brought home a few leftover candies for my sisters, they would know I had been given more than my fair share. Either way I might have to concede that it was not a myth that I was my father's favourite.

It is entirely possible I am making this up. When you tell a story often enough it begins to feel true, and I have told this one many times before. Imagination mixes with memory as we get older, and I am now over seventy, an old woman for sure. Still, I remember that, on that day, my anxieties about sibling rivalry became secondary to my anxiety about the fact that my father had vanished, that he had abandoned me. I was left with several stark choices. It was possible that the Second Coming had happened and that he had been taken up into glory. It was also possible that he had dropped down dead, another way of going to heaven. But I did not let myself even think about that. The least frightening conclusion by far was that he had simply disappeared around the curving surface of the earth. That would fit with what I had learned in Roseville School.

I chose to believe that the earth is round. With that belief came also the lifelong comfort of accepting that my father's death, on July 29, 1976, was a part of the life that goes on. This lesson serves me well now. As I age and confront my own mortality, I consciously try to imitate my father's stoicism. He often recited to himself a version of the serenity prayer: *"Wass ich nicht ändern kann, nehm ich geduldig an, meiner Zufriedenheit."* What I cannot change I accept patiently for the sake of my peace. Believing that the earth is round is like accepting a gift from my father. Colour the last bead green and, as you do so, imagine the peace of knowing that both life and death go on, that when our species dies out, our green planet will keep on going round and round. All of us, including my father and me, will be like Wordsworth's Lucy: "Rolled round in earth's diurnal course / With rocks, and stones, and trees."

GO FOR IT: WRITING MY FATHER'S STORY

*by **Julia Spicher Kasdorf***

The story my father tells about himself begins like this: "As an Amish boy growing up in Big Valley, I always wondered what was on the other side of the mountain."

Sometimes he adds that he listened for train whistles in the distance, but did not see a locomotive until he was much older. He describes the tramps who walked in the dirt lane, having ridden that invisible railroad through the Ridge and Valley region of central Pennsylvania and somehow found his family's farm. His parents enjoyed talking with those worldly men who sometimes smelled of booze and who ate his mother's meals with great gusto on the porch. Afterward, she boiled their plates and silverware against tuberculosis, but she contracted it anyway, weakened as she was from overwork. The tramps were welcome to sleep in the barn as long as they surrendered their cigarettes and matches against the threat of fire.

As a boy, Dad tells us, he fell from the overden, a loft about eight metres above the barn floor, and lay unconscious on a living room davenport for most of the night. He suffered seizures until his parents took him out of the valley to a Pennsylvania Dutch folk healer, called a "pow wow doctor," who chanted medieval German charms with appeals to the Holy Trinity over the injury; then he recovered. Less frequently, he tells how his toddler brother drowned in the watering trough. And then, how the barn burned down at milking time. His tubercular mother watched the conflagration from the house; she was quarantined in an upstairs bedroom, having struck a deal with the doctor who wanted to send her away to a sanatorium: no house-work, all five children banned from her room until she gained strength and weight. When she was finally able to get out, she and her sister Mary and all the children—aged two to fifteen—were involved in the horse and buggy accident that broke her neck and ended her life two days later.

One summer, teaching English as a second language to refugees, it occurred to me to ask Dad how he learned to speak English. On the first day of school, he said, he was told to stand in the corner because he could not understand the teacher's instructions. It was hard to learn in that disorderly, one-room public school, and he was forbidden to practice at home. And it was hard to learn English all over again the next fall, after forgetting over the summer. I don't know when it occurred to me to place his narrative beside the fact that our people had been living on American soil since the 1730s. All those years of silent, stubborn separation. Classmates threw his black felt Sunday hat down the hole in the outhouse, and non-Amish people yelled "Conchie" and threw rotten tomatoes at his father as the two of them rode a spring wagon through town during the Second World War. In his primary and secondary years, he skipped classes to help plant and harvest the crops.

In my dad's teen years, my grandfather chose to remarry a Conservative Conference Mennonite woman; he joined her church and learned how to drive. That's how quickly change can happen in a family, in a small community that began as a single Amish settlement but that now contains more stripes of Anabaptism than anywhere else in the world—most of them relatives. Thus, my grandfather offered Dad a new car at age sixteen if he would drop out of school and inherit a farm. Dad chose to stay in high school and go on to a Mennonite college, against his father's warning that higher education would surely make him *grosshensich* (big-headed) like J.W. Yoder, the Amish-born musician and author who also came from that valley. During the 1950s in the United States, almost anything was possible with education, especially in the sciences.

All of these stories I have written in some form, my lyric machine humming in their silences, interpreting ambiguities, filling gaps to make the poems I needed to comfort myself and organize the chaotic life my father didn't entirely choose and couldn't help. I've worked them into essays that tell and contradict and then retell the stories again, fashioning narratives more coherent than anything that actually happened.

My dad enrolled in a medical college in Richmond, Virginia, and when he arrived in that capital of the Confederacy was scolded by a stranger for drinking from a "coloured" fountain. In June, he returned to the valley to wed his Mennonite high school sweetheart; her uncle, the bishop who married them, was carried out of the reception, dead on an ambulance stretcher. While my father studied in Richmond, my mother worked as a registered nurse in the Negro wards. During their second year of marriage, she was severely burned in a stove fire in their apartment and hospitalized for three months. When she was released, their one-year-old son no longer recognized her. In his third year of studies, my father was expelled for poor academic performance. Years later, when the grown-up son interviewed at the same institution, he learned that our father was the only northerner in his class, a cultural outsider disliked by some faculty and possibly dismissed for that reason.

But we learned that only years later. What could my parents do then but take their losses and failures home to Big Valley? Still in their twenties, they were both motherless, expecting another baby, and deeply in debt. Mercifully, my father got work in a research laboratory at a medical centre some distance away. This meant that he was absent during the weeks while my mother cared for their toddler and her recently widowed father, and that he was not on hand to drive my mother to the hospital for my birth. Before I turned one, we moved out of the valley.

Growing up, I absorbed the griefs they carried but rarely named and also their determined perseverance. Only much later did I see in their experience a critique of the "happily ever after" stories that perfume the air little girls breathe. Maybe that is why I refused those fairy tales, choosing instead to reflect on the heroic distance my father had come: from plowing with horses to the Westinghouse Research and Development Center. My midcentury modern father wore suits and ties and carried a briefcase, every day driving to "the R&D," a complex so important we could not follow him past the security guard's booth. And he continued to travel, flying in and out of Pittsburgh International Airport with its massive Calder mobile, gone for several days at a time, or even a week sometimes. On one early trip, he stayed up all night riding city buses in Chicago, just to see the marvellous city.

My two brothers and I were also urged to "go for it," as if success were a distant destination. Success required a departure, and we were poised to take off like rockets. For as long as I can remember, my parents asked, "What are your goals?" Not pressure exactly, but an expectation to "do your best," to "stand up, shoulders back, speak slowly and distinctly," as Mom often reminded us. Abilities are gifts from God, and faithful living meant making the most of ourselves. Mom celebrated small successes around the dinner table by filling fancy teacups with grape juice. Once, at a family reunion, our family performed a skit for the talent show in which each of us children came home to report an accomplishment—a part in the school play or place on the honour roll—and were treated to the obnoxious parental refrain suggestive of upward mobility: "Spichers come out on top!" After the final delivery of that punchline, my father bowed to the audience and ripped off his toupée. I now realize I still report personal accomplishments like small trophies I bring home to present to my parents, who had gone for it and earned mixed results.

Where did it come from—such unbridled ambition and optimism, despite my parents' experience to the contrary? Was it just the air one breathed in the United States back then, or were there other sources? I recall references to *The Power of Positive Thinking*, Norman Vincent Peale's combination of Reformed theology and self-help psychology, which sold five million copies and remained on the *New York Times* bestseller list for 186 consecutive weeks in the early 1950s. The New York City preacher also published *Guideposts*, cheerful devotional booklets I often saw atop toilet tanks or bedside tables in Mennonite homes. Dale Carnegie died in 1955, but I'm certain his classic, *How to Win Friends and Influence People*, occupied a place in my parents' library. And among my first memories of Mennonite worship were meetings in a classroom at the University of Pittsburgh, then the basement of an urban synagogue, then a house purchased by early members of what became Pittsburgh Mennonite Church. Now I admire the confidence evident in that kind of improvisation. All his life my father continued to follow the latest theories of corporate management, self-improvement, and popular theology, as if distinction—and salvation—could be obtained by anyone through hard work and study.

But for all that striving, Dad also demonstrated our duty to return to and honour our original community. We saw him struggle to speak Pennsylvania Dutch with his uncles at family funerals or visits in their plain homes. With genuine curiosity he asked his brothers about the herd of dairy cows on the home farm or the sheep and chickens at the other farm. "We are the ones who left, so we know something about their world," he once told me, "but they are not obligated to care about ours." But he said next to nothing about the loss that comes from leaving. When we were young, my brothers and I spent summer months on relatives' farms in Big Valley, and so of course I thought I loved that place more than the industrialized rural landscape outside Pittsburgh where I grew up.

During my teenage years, Dad was part of the Westinghouse team that redesigned laboratories at the Johns Hopkins Hospital. He invited me to accompany him on one of those trips. While he worked, I spent a day in the Walters Art Museum and exploring the historic Mount Vernon neighbourhood of Baltimore. After a city dinner, as we passed through the lobby of the hotel, he advised me to walk a few steps ahead of him so people wouldn't think I was his mistress. Why do I remember that moment so clearly? The warning came as a shock, simultaneously revealing as much about the worldly world as about my father's careful consciousness; he was the alien and stranger, always mindful of appearance and his tenuous position. It also revealed something about the complexity of real life: in order to avoid the appearance of evil, I needed to perform a small deception. At the same time, it underscored the sexual difference that would always divide us.

When I was young, our relationship seemed simple: I admired him and he adored me, the engine of our mutual affection fuelled by his glamorous absences and my Saturday morning baking of sweets. (I still make him chocolate pecan pies laced with amaretto whenever I can.) He called me

"Jules," a boy's name for the girl stuck in the middle of the Chevy's back seat between older Jim and younger Jeff. He held my hand on Sunday-afternoon walks with my brothers as he taught us the names of trees, plants, birds, and flowers, whatever caught his eyes in the scrubby woods that was an overgrown farm on the hill above our home. Mom stayed in the house and napped. Now I can guess that she needed a break, with him away so much, at the R&D or, as she said, "out of town on business." Evenings, I helped him in the garden while we discussed big things beyond our home: The Mafia, The Communists, and The Mennonite Church.

Such uncomplicated love I would not come to feel for my mother until I hit fifty. She was the taken-for-granted presence in the house, enforcer of cultural expectations and teacher of domestic skills, moral obligations, and sexual rules and roles. As an only daughter, I was all the eggs in one basket, and I knew they'd better stay perfectly unbroken. She taught me to clean, cook, and bake; sew, mend, and iron; can, freeze, and pickle; to pursue beauty, especially in one's personal appearance and home interior; and to do all things with ferocious thrift. "A woman can throw out in a teaspoon what a man makes in a week," she quoted her mother. When I was thirteen, she enrolled me in the sort of charm school one got in southwestern Pennsylvania, sponsored by the YWCA and conducted in the basement of a Methodist Church. There I learned the proper ways to walk, sit, eat, apply makeup, refuse chewing gum, and make everyone feel comfortable, which is charm's goal, in addition to attracting an ambitious Mennonite husband. She called me by the name my father had vetoed at my birth, "Julianna Rose," after the queen of the Netherlands.

Early on, I must have observed that women in our family could end up sick in the bedroom or injured in the kitchen or dead. To go for it, I'd need to follow the men—or marry the right man—but how to handle the complexities of sexuality? During the summer of 1983, as a college student, I worked on the daily newssheet for the Mennonite General Assembly, a joint convention of the Mennonite Church and General Conference convened at Bethlehem, Pennsylvania, to celebrate three hundred years of Mennonites in North America. One morning I ventured out in tan sandals with wedge heels, an Indian-print wrap-around skirt, and a black peasant top that was loose but sheerer, perhaps, than I had realized in my dim hotel room. I ran into Dad in the parking lot of the arena where the main assembly met, and we engaged in a short, inconsequential conversation. When I encountered my mother later, however, she told me with some anxiety that my father had reported I was not wearing all my underwear that day, and I had better find a brassiere! I still feel the shame and mortification of my twenty-year-old self.

For all the distance he had come, Dad remained an Amish boy from Big Valley, raised in a communal culture to be highly attuned to the unspoken judgments of others, boundlessly ambitious, yet modest to the point of embarrassment.

During the 1970s, lacking credentials but swept along by his smarts, deferential humility, and work ethic, Dad collaborated with engineers with degrees from MIT. He argued the virtues of nuclear power, even after Three Mile Island, and described enormous turbines and fantastic schemes to harness the tides to produce electricity. During the twentieth century, Westinghouse engineers and scientists were granted more than twenty-eight thousand government patents for the inventions of things like the X-ray tube, the atomic clock, and the flat-screen TV—third among all US corporations. At the end of the year, R&D researchers celebrated their having won more patents for their inventions than the team at General Electric, even though GE had more employees. When we stood on Mount Washington at night and gazed down on the Golden Triangle glimmering at the confluence of Pittsburgh's three rivers, we proudly watched the Westinghouse sign—which is no longer there—on the north shore, a row of the "circle W" corporate insignia illuminating in endless variation through the genius of the world's first computer-driven sign. Dad claimed that his favourite colour was a distinct shade of periwinkle called "Westinghouse blue."

When Ronald Reagan took office and immediately removed Jimmy Carter's solar panels from the White House roof, calling them "a joke," Department of Defense research contracts replaced contracts from the Department of Energy. Dad had followed federal funding shifts from health care to energy research, but as a Mennonite he could not in good conscience develop weapons. Nor, I suppose, could he imagine leaving a company that had provided him with a professional identity and financial security. Endlessly earning his place in the R&D, he sometimes worked long days or Saturday mornings, explaining that professionals do not punch clocks—now

I see that farmers don't either, but they stay close to home. In order to keep a position at Westinghouse during the 1980s, Dad pursued graduate work in industrial hygiene and turned his sights to keeping R&D scientists safe. On the perfectly landscaped, 150-acre campus of forty buildings, he logged the uranium that passed in and out of labs and managed the cleanup of a PCB spill in a nearby creek.

Mainly Dad's workplace produced secrets, so I was not allowed to see inside his office until 1999, when I happened to spend the fall semester as a visiting poet at the University of Pittsburgh. By then, Westinghouse Corporation had collapsed, and he was one of the last employees left in that massive facility. He held high-level security clearance and knew the history of the nuclear reactor's meltdown, as well as how to handle the disposal of hazardous materials. He invited me to join him for lunch in the employee cafeteria one afternoon, warmly greeting me in the lobby of a building made entirely of black glass with a roadway tunnelling through. He led me down a silent corridor, gesturing through open doors to empty laboratories: "That's where they worked on...." "In there we made...." Eventually, we reached a series of offices and desks: "That's where the receptionist sat. My secretary worked there. That was my boss's office." In a small conference room next to his office, an evacuation map of the Pittsburgh area covered the entire wall, concentric circles radiating out from the R&D, a squat rotary phone on the table.

In my father's story—and what achingly binds his life to mine—I see the narrative of wonder and curiosity, risk and work, departure and loss. His mythic life begins with speaking a largely unwritten tongue and follows the modern rise and fall of the United States from the Great Depression to post-war prosperity and opportunity to inevitable calamity. We make choices without fully understanding their consequences. What we believe are decisions are not really choices at all, driven as we are by our insatiable natures—bound as we are to react in the best ways we can to the unexpected crises that constitute everyday life.

When I sent my father an essay I'd written about his childhood encounters with tramps, based on lecture notes he'd prepared on the topic but elaborated on by my own imagining, he replied, "This is what creative writing is? You just get to say whatever you want?"

Perhaps it is no wonder that my father suffered when I wrote and published his stories. At once pleased with my success, he is vexed by its means. Not only have I made unseemly private things public, but half the time I have gotten the details wrong. A man of science, he knows truth to be material, discernable through observation and replication, not something we fabricate from unreliable memories and desire. For this reason, expressions of popular Christianity both fascinate and confound him, raised as he was to believe less in claims of personal salvation and more in the material reality of labour, the spiritual reality of hope, and the redemption of communal belonging. Whatever the reason, he—along with my entire family: nurse mother, physician older brother, nursing professor younger brother—favours non-fiction, or perhaps non-creative non-fiction, by which I mean information, just the facts please.

Drafting this essay in the early weeks of Donald Trump's presidency in the United States, I cannot help but feel a fresh appreciation for verifiable detail. Before the inauguration of this man who calls global climate change a "hoax invented by the Chinese," climate scientists on my campus scrambled to stockpile data on foreign servers. PEN America now must fight to protect the dignity of American journalists who strive to report real news. When I sent a copy of this essay home to my father for fact checking, he did not argue with my interpretations, but confined his comments to literal details: the hat in the outhouse was black felt, not straw. Nor have I asserted dramatic interpretations or insisted on the truth of my memory. Furthermore, writing this essay has compelled me to consider the invention and collaboration inherent in scientific research. This is what creative writing is: another kind of R&D.

Canadian and Russian Mennonite author Rudy Wiebe recently reminded me of the first time he met my father. Rudy and I had driven together to Eastern Mennonite University, my father's alma mater, where the distinguished novelist had been invited to give a reading. Afterward, he said something to my dad about having "a poet for a daughter," to which Dad sheepishly replied, "We mustn't get proud." Rudy was so surprised by this "Amish" response that to this day he cannot tell the story without laughing.

So, I will write a happy ending. For one thing, I am thankful that my parents are both alive and in relatively good health. Recently, Mom told me she cannot believe her youngest son just turned fifty; she is just so surprised and grateful! My father, always more inclined to worry, wonders whether they can afford to live so long, having outlasted their own parents by decades. (Of course they can.) And he has begun to write his own story, already insisting that it must differ from the self-published solipsistic memoirs of his friends. I haven't seen much of it yet, but I mail him used copies of books like Louise DeSalvo's *Writing as a Way of Healing*. With his usual cocktail of ambition and humility, he likes to tell people the story of how he mistyped his working title, *Peering into the Memory Box*, omitting the "r" in the first word.

As for myself, I live with my little family in a little house over the mountains from Big Valley, fewer than fifty kilometres from where my father was born, still earning my place at a research university known mostly for engineering and the sciences. Much of the time, my life feels like an impossible improvisation; every August, for instance, when I should be writing syllabi for the next semester's poetry workshops, I decide to can quarts and quarts of peaches and tomatoes in a steaming kitchen. My current writing project attempts to make visible some of the people and places harmed by fracking for natural gas in Pennsylvania and argues for the development of sustainable energy sources. I would like to believe I have moved on to writing about other things, but I recognize that this work also continues my father's story.

REFLECTIONS OF A GRATEFUL DAUGHTER

*by **Carol Dyck***

Sometimes, when I was a teenager, my father would drive me to school and we would enjoy lovely grown-up conversations. But I remember, in particular, one of these mornings. The night before I had stayed out very late, and when I got home my dad was beside himself with worry; so he disciplined me in anger. He spoke loudly to me. He was worried because as a physician he dealt with many pregnant teenage girls and *his* fear was that I would ruin my life. He really had no reason to fear. I learned the facts of life from the clinical obstetrics text he left open on his desk. A great way to make a girl think twice! At the same time, *my* fear was that all that stress would ruin his health. That night I wept because he was so tired and I had made him worry. The next morning, as we drove to school, he apologized to me. It was a very tender moment. Whatever his shortcomings as a father may have been, he was kind and I loved him, and because of that, I was willing to forgive him for almost anything.

My father, Abraham Bernard Voth (1914–1989), was born and raised on a farm near Hepburn, Saskatchewan. He finished school, attended Bible school, and then trained as a schoolteacher. For several years he taught biology and chemistry at the Mennonite Educational Institute in Clearbrook, British Columbia. Although he was a wonderful teacher, he had really always wanted to be a doctor. However, after the war, spaces in Canadian medical schools were reserved for veterans. It was not until after I was born that he was accepted into the medical program at the University of Saskatchewan. And so, with a wife and two daughters to support, he went back to school. After graduating, he became a general practitioner. He held regular office hours to see patients in the afternoons, and in the mornings he was at the hospital making his rounds, performing all kinds of surgeries and administering anesthetics. In his "spare time" he made house calls, and at all hours of the day and night he delivered babies. Amazingly, over the course of his career he delivered two generations of babies.

Both of my parents came from large combined families. Widows and widowers would get together and bring their children together, and then sometimes as a new couple they would have more children. This was the case for both sets of my grandparents. Therefore, I have lots of relatives. I didn't get to know many of them very well, unfortunately. However, I do have fairly strong memories of our annual visits to the country at Christmastime to visit grandparents, aunts and uncles, and cousins. December 25 belonged to my mother's family, and December 26 to my father's side.

For many people, Boxing Day brings thoughts of bargains and long shopping lines. For me it brings the memory of our annual thirty-mile journey from Saskatoon to my grandfather's farm near Hepburn, Saskatchewan. This farm had no electricity, running water, or plumbing. There was a tiny house where my sister and I shared confined spaces with cousins we barely knew. And there was an outhouse! I had denied myself all liquids for days in preparation for this event because I refused to use this outside toilet in below-zero temperatures. There was also a barn, and at some point in the afternoon my grandfather took the uncles out to the barn to "check the horses." I eventually realized that this was not because of any concern he had for the horses, but because he had a still in the barn for making spirits. I wonder if these sorts of spirit-filled visits to the barn happened at other Mennonite family gatherings, too.

My father occasionally told me things about his father. One of them was that he had often been cruel to his animals. I did not find that hard to believe. My grandfather was a rather wild-looking man with grungy overalls and uncombed hair. As a child I thought he was perhaps incapable of speech, because he had a very low, growly voice with which he uttered Low German phrases that I didn't understand. In fact, I never had an actual conversation with him. I would look at him, and at the dowdy farm, and I could hardly believe that this was where my father grew up.

I have never seen my father dishevelled. Sweatpants and T-shirts were definitely not his style. He was always dressed impeccably. He had a dignity that seemed completely natural to him, so who had modelled this for him? Perhaps, like so many of *our* children, he modelled himself in opposition to his parental examples.

My father was careful and meticulous in his thinking as well. This made him a great teacher. I still meet former students of his who tell me how much they had admired him. As a doctor, he loved his work. He was a skilled practitioner and a calm and gentle man with a very compassionate bedside manner.

He was a wonderful person, but I have to admit he was not always a perfect father. He missed events that were important to me, like my grade twelve graduation ceremony, because he was busy taking care of other people. He often gave me a cheque for Christmas when I would have preferred a gift he had chosen for me. He was away so much that he sometimes missed cues regarding my health that should have been noticed and looked after.

My father was also not unaffected by society's accepted ideas and practices with regard to gender roles, and this was at times apparent within our family. He would decide on family vacations without consulting his wife or his daughters. He would come home with a new car to surprise us all. Major purchases like these were not necessarily discussed with us beforehand. He would also bring home things for our home that really didn't reflect my mother's taste. For instance, I remember the statue of a nearly naked Greek woman on a pedestal that he brought home to put in our living room. Needless to say, we didn't have guests for some time after that. Eventually, the woman disappeared and something else was placed on her pedestal.

His unconscious acceptance of contemporary gendered language was somewhat apparent in his workplace as well. He referred to the secretary and nurse in his office as "the girls." They were, in fact, fine, mature Mennonite women who were also our friends. Indeed, the office staff and their families, my parents included, occasionally went on vacations together and enjoyed one another's company. The nurse who helped him set up his first office retired when he did twenty-five years later, so there was obviously a firm basis for mutual respect, in spite of the terminology used.

And as a daughter I always felt respected by my father. He spoke to me as an adult even when I was quite young, making me believe in my own abilities and intelligence. He wanted me to go into medicine, like he had. So I worked in his office in summer when his staff took vacations. I learned to perform small procedures, like taking blood samples from people's fingers. And sometimes I just watched him. This practice of allowing me to observe him performing sometimes less-than-pretty mini-surgeries, however, eventually proved counterproductive to his vocational aspirations for me. It was after I watched him pull out an infected ingrown toenail that I realized medicine was not for me.

My father was a professional person who operated within a fairly wide cultural context, but I can't think about him apart from his Mennonite roots. They shaped him and also influenced my life. My parents both grew up in small Mennonite towns where they were, in fact, physically separated from the non-Mennonite world. They were even separate from other kinds of Mennonites. My mother grew up in the General Conference Mennonite town of Langham, Saskatchewan. It was a safe twenty miles distant from my father's Mennonite Brethren town of Hepburn. They met in the common ground of city life in Saskatoon, and when my mother married my father, she had to "convert" to the Mennonite Brethren Conference, the road to heaven was that narrow. In the city they lost that literal physical separation from "the world," but social and religious separations were still part of their thinking. In time, my father's religious world gradually widened to accept the legitimacy of other Mennonites and non-Mennonite evangelicals, and eventually he opened his arms even wider to affirm other Christian denominations. In fact, he became an international board member of the Christian Business Men's Association.

The impact of the "separation" ethos on me was very strong. For my parents their school and church environments had been similar. The same values, the same behaviours, even the same people were involved in both. For me they were not. For example, the social life of my school often revolved around dances. Unwritten but clearly understood religious rules, such as the prohibition of dancing, caused endless embarrassment for me and kept me from being fully involved in my school community. I dropped out of a prestigious club I was invited to join in high school when I learned that part of its role was to plan the school dances. I really wanted to be in that club, but I refused to put myself in a position where I would have to say that it was "against my religion" to dance. I loved dancing and I saw nothing wrong with it. To me, the taboo against dancing was just another way the church tried to keep us from forming relationships with non-Christians, to keep us "separate." This type of legalism created a deep dissonance between what I believed in my heart and what I agreed to theoretically as a Mennonite.

When it comes to religion and spiritual issues, there are many forces that shape us. Our family didn't practice any specific religious practices or rituals within the home. If my parents prayed together at night, I certainly never overheard them. We never read devotional books before meals. Table grace was assigned to us girls, and we sped through our prayers at breakneck speed until even we couldn't recognize what we were saying. But we went to church every Sunday, and we were all involved in one way or another.

My father was involved in church life in various ways, as a Sunday school teacher, a council member, and occasionally a preacher. In the early days he preached on the *Gospel Tidings* radio program. And of course, he was always a generous donor to the church.

As for me, I was invited to join the church choir when I was in grade six. As a teenager I taught Sunday school, was a member of the youth group council, and eventually led a children's choir. In many ways, the church was a good place for me. I made wonderful friends there; I was also given many opportunities to develop my skills.

On the other hand, if there was a patriarchal influence in my life, it was the church. Although I didn't notice it at the time, it was strictly male in its leadership, with limited participation of women outside of the kitchen. As I learned later, there were actual rules about what women could and could not do in church, but the cultural assumptions of the day alone were strong enough to keep things at the societal status quo. As a child I never questioned those assumptions.

Also, as a child I never questioned the dominant theological story. Personal salvation was the primary focus of our theology. There were certain words you had to say; you had to accept Jesus into your heart so that you would go to heaven and be saved from hell. Certainly it was in church where I heard sermons about hell that gave me "fire dreams." As a child, I burned in all conceivable ways in my dreams. It was in church that I was taught the dire consequences of not believing exactly what I was told. If I were to think or imagine anything outside of the church's specific spiritual box, I would burn forever. God had strict rules about the matter.

"Witnessing" was the next priority. That is, you were expected to speak about your religion with a view to converting other people. After high school I spent an entire summer in Europe with *Missions* and *Youth for Christ* doing exactly that. When it was over, I was overwhelmed with the shallowness of the experience, and promised myself I would not do that again. I couldn't accept the idea that you were "born again" in order to procreate, to make more Christians. There had to be more to the Christian life than that. It was my father who paid for me and a friend to do this, but I have long since forgiven him for sending me there.

Thankfully I worked on the youth group committee with a young medical student who had been given the gift of doubt. He showed me that it was possible to argue with and analyze biblical teachings. He showed me the joy of interacting with sacred text in more complex ways than simply "believing." He saved my life in the church.

I regret that during my youth I heard very little about the Mennonite distinctive beliefs of peace making and social justice. When I later learned that these had been long-standing concerns of the Mennonite community, I felt a new kinship to the church; I could be proud of these kinds of priorities.

And what part did my father play in my youthful absorption of the church's view of God? That is difficult to know, exactly. We didn't discuss religious ideas at home. There was little or no overlap of language between church and home, which makes it hard for me to understand how I implicitly understood that my parents were in accord with the influence of the church in my life. Perhaps because of this language disconnect between home and church, I rarely shared my religious questions with my father. I wish I had, but in truth I shared my heretical thoughts only with my diary. On the positive side, whatever my church language lacked in terms of an emphasis on peace or social justice, I learned from my father's life. I learned true concern and caring from him in the way he took care of people. I learned generosity and gentleness, which are the foundational principles of my faith to this day. I will always be grateful to him for this.

Perhaps the greatest effect my father had on my spiritual life occurred when I was fifteen years old. My best friend and I were manipulated into a "conversion" experience at the end of a week of "deeper life" meetings. The guest preacher met us at the door and confronted us in front of all of our friends on our need for salvation. He pleaded with us to go downstairs to pray with him. Thoroughly embarrassed, we both burst into tears. Unfortunately I was not yet fluent in the language of argument, so we went downstairs with him. He did all the praying; we did all the crying. When it was over I was livid, but then my father put his arms around me and told me how happy he was. This was a crisis for me. There was no way I was going to disappoint him. So I worked at adjusting my attitude and decided I had better try to make this real in some way. It was not the easiest entry into the kingdom.

My father gave himself unsparingly to helping people who were ill, until finally he paid the price for his continuous exhaustion and succumbed to illness himself. It began with a strong allergy to surgical gloves, limiting his ability to work.

Then he developed a severe case of asthma and became allergic to all but a few kinds of food. He broke ribs coughing and had to sit up in a chair many nights to get any sleep at all. Most heartbreakingly of all, he fell into a serious clinical depression. This came with the realization that in all the years of treating depression in his patients, he had never completely understood how powerless depressed people were to find peace and happiness. In the end, he died a slow and painful death from bowel cancer. I had always seen him as a very strong person; it was difficult for me to see him in such a state of weakness.

The last years of my father's life were heavy and dark. Those painful last impressions of him are often still very vivid for me. But writing this piece has given me an opportunity to look back past those years to enjoy simple, happy, and humorous memories of my earlier years with Dad.

Fathers and daughters do not always see things from the same perspective, and that can lead to some humorous situations. For example, when I was in high school, I needed a complete physical exam for some reason. I had no regular doctor—in fact, I had never even been to see a doctor—so my father made an appointment for me with someone he knew. As I was lying on the examining table with nothing but a thin paper sheet over me, my father's choice of a doctor walked in. To my horror this was a young man I knew socially. He frequently came to our house for Christian Medical Association parties. I had never found out his last name so I hadn't made the connection. I guess when you look at naked people in your office every day, you can forget that young teenaged girls can feel a little self-conscious about a situation like this! Oh, Dad, what were you thinking?

Sometimes our family life looked like a TV sitcom. For instance, in my house you needed a strong stomach because often, during mealtimes, we were regaled with stories of horrible car accidents and burn victims. But this was simply my father sharing his day with us. And then there were the celebratory dinners, when we ate turkey. Dad would hold the carving knife like a scalpel and "perform surgery," naming all the pertinent body parts and muscle tissues as he went. In the end, we were all keenly aware of the bird as a body and I had lost all interest in eating it. To this day I have difficulty touching meat; these are the scars we carry through life.

My dad had a sweet and affectionate side. I attended the Mennonite Brethren Bible College (MBBC) in Winnipeg for two years. During that time, I think I was the only student who got mail every day. That was because at the end of his workday, Dad would write to me on a "Beautiful Saskatoon" postcard and send it out with the office mail. He spoke of simple things— funny stories from his day, like the woman from the country who brought in a full quart sealer of urine to be tested. Or about happenings in the church community, or what my three young nieces were up to.

Probably many people saw my father as a very serious person, but he actually had a lovely sense of humour. Dad loved his boats and he loved Waskesiu Lake; we went there many times as a family. On one of those trips my sister, having just met up with some friends, asked Dad if she could take the car for a drive. She had just gotten her licence and was quite excited about driving. Dad said yes. The road we took became a trail and then an ever-narrowing path. There was a terrible moment when the car stalled and she couldn't get it to move. We were stuck between two trees! The rest of us girls got out and tried to bend the trees out of the way. No luck. So my sister gunned the motor and forced the car through the trees, wrecking all four doors in the process. We drove fearfully back to face our parents, but my dad just chuckled. (My mother did not!) Apparently he could see humour where others couldn't. All the doors had to be replaced.

My father had no formal musical education, but he learned to love classical music. When I took a university course on symphonic music, I was amazed at how many themes I remembered from hearing them constantly throughout my childhood. And later, I remember leaving our two children with my parents for a week when they were four and six years old. Every night during that week, my father sat in a big chair with our four-year-old son, Adrian, and the two of them listened to a particular Rachmaninoff recording. Long after we had returned home, Adrian would sing bits of those themes over the phone for his beloved grandpa. I think that was one of the experiences that led Adrian to love music enough to choose it as a career.

I know that my father was proud of me. We weren't a physically demonstrative family and we didn't often say words like "I love you," but Dad had other ways of showing his love and pride. For example, when I was practising for my grade ten piano exam, he recorded me so that I could listen to myself and improve my playing. One day a friend of mine visited his office and while sitting in the waiting room she heard piano music playing. When she saw my dad, he asked her if she had noticed the piano music and told her proudly that it was me playing. I heard similar stories from several other patients of his as well.

My parents were always supportive, and they would travel anywhere to hear me sing. In 1966 I had a solo part consisting of about twenty-five notes sung as an echo in a major choral work performed by the MBBC Choir and the Winnipeg Symphony Orchestra. They flew out to hear me. Later, when I began composing music, they would come to Edmonton to support me. I was writing music that combined choral anthems with solo songs, and I usually sang the soprano solos. It was heartwarming for me to experience not only their enjoyment of my singing, but also their awe at realizing that I had written this music.

In general, thinking about my father's life, I realize how far he moved during his lifetime, how much he changed and developed. For his generation, the circumstances of the world changed dramatically in a relatively short period of time. He always seemed to manage the adjustments that so much change required. However, depression challenged the very fibre of his being. He spoke about how it affected his faith and about the accommodations he was having to make. I hope that if he is watching from above, he will understand the accommodations that I have made as well. I still count on his kindness and generosity.

At his death, I wrote in his obituary: "To his family he was always a hero, saving lives and healing wounds on a daily basis. He dreamed extravagantly and relentlessly pursued his dreams."

OUR LIVES TOGETHER, MY FATHER AND ME

by *Hildi Froese Tiessen*

What remains most palpably for me of my father are images, vignettes. Seeing him resting on one knee beside a dusty road at the margin of a field to inspect heads of ripening grain, rubbing the kernels between his palms as I knew even then he must have done many times before. I could feel the sacramental quality of those unexpected interludes, though I really had no way of knowing what they actually meant for him. It would be a sunny August afternoon, inevitably a Sunday. We'd be on a trip into the country to visit my aunts and uncles who farmed on the southern Manitoba prairie where he, too, tenaciously and in uncertain circumstances, had for some twenty years worked the land. It was usually just the three of us on these trips—my father and mother and me—while my four older siblings, more or less oblivious of me in any case, carried on their lives back home, in the northeast neighbourhoods of Winnipeg, where our family had settled in the spring of 1951. My siblings, teenagers by then, had spent their early years on isolated prairie farms from which they had travelled several kilometres to one-room schools—by horse-drawn sled or by bicycle or on foot—and had been compelled to negotiate a world strikingly different from the urban landscape in which I grew up. In fact, one of my brothers remarked that I had been something of an only child. My two brothers, the eldest among us, were very close companions and my two sisters were the best of friends as well. I was the youngest by five years.

There were also trips into the country in spring, when the Manitoba gumbo, following substantial rains, would make rural roads next to impassable. I held my breath while my father accelerated enough to coax our car forward, balancing the need for torque with the risk of losing control while he negotiated the deep, twisty, gummy ruts. In spite of the intense sense of urgency these episodes evoked in me, my father, for whom this was familiar ground, seemed to operate matter-of-factly, and I remember being impressed by his courage, resolve, and skill in swinging the steering wheel authoritatively back and forth in wide arcs while the car lurched and swayed. It was both frightening and exhilarating. There were no exclamations when it was all over. That sort of commentary was not part of our vernacular. We simply carried on.

Those tended to be magical trips for me. In those days before seat belts, I would stretch out in the back of the car on the hour-long return to the city and fall asleep to the murmurs of my parents' conversation. I would be awakened by the stops and turns that suggested we were getting close to home, and by the lights of the city, denoting landmarks I might have recognized, had I sat up to take notice. I felt very much protected and loved when days like that came to an end. Neither coddled nor neglected. Just comfortable, secure.

There was surely a lot more going on in my father's life than I was inclined or able to comprehend in those days, the late 1950s and early '60s. But some things struck me even then, gave me pause. Like his muffled voice behind a closed bedroom door the afternoon I came home when I was around fourteen and cautiously reported to my mother that I had found bloodstains on my underwear. I barely knew what to make of that (no one had prepared me for the event, really, though I seemed to have some kind of intuitive understanding of what was going on and was not unduly distressed). Soon after my mother heard my news she went into the next room, where she must have told my dad. My most vivid memory of the whole episode was my father's audible, apparently incredulous exclamation, in Low German, which was the language of their conversation: "*Ney!*" ("No!")—which made me think that my news had greater import than I had initially realized. I wonder now what must have been going through his mind when he came to realize so abruptly that his youngest was on the cusp of no longer being a child. He would have been about fifty then, and would live close to another forty years.

The voice that uttered that exclamation was inclined to erupt precipitously, most often in response to some irritant that evoked for my dad emotions that seemingly could be neither contained nor dispelled in any other way. I've often thought that my own proclivity to offer rash outbursts rather than prudent, judicious remarks about matters that unsettle me was inherited from him. I continue to work to ameliorate that tendency to react explosively, and I am mindful of the fact that the caution I try to practice in the face of such volatility is surely at work even now, here, in the tenor and trajectory of this tentative reflection about our lives together, my father and me.

Ah. My father's voice. It was one of the notable traces he left. We kids heard it, steady and pious, at daily devotions around the breakfast table. And in the evening, when any number of the five of us might create a bit of tension, disagreeing loudly with one another about this or that. We knew that even while our boisterousness swelled he would remain quiet—but only for so long. Eventually he would explode, never lashing out physically, but making it eminently clear that whatever was going on was now at an end. And when he made his voice heard, that surely was the end of it.

And then there was his insistent summons on a Saturday morning. Baking day. My mother would begin early to prepare any or all of *Zwieback* and *Bulkje*, *Stretsel*, *Platz*, *Perieschje*, muffins and cakes. We girls—my sisters in their teens, and me almost there—loved to sleep in. But there was work to do, maybe something as simple as washing the kitchen floor or transferring pans of pastries into or out of the oven while my parents went out to shop. So we slept in—until the call came up the stairs. We were addressed in Low German then: pressing, demanding: "*Mejales!*" That three-syllable

Low German expression for "girls" certainly conveyed greater urgency than its English or High German equivalents. It was a fairly constant Saturday morning alarm.

In my early years, and then later maybe only on Sundays (because his weekday morning began before mine), I heard my father's morning prayer at the breakfast table. It followed his reading from the *Kalenderblatt* so popular among Mennonite Brethren (MB) families in those days: a tear-off calendar, each page featuring a Bible verse accompanied by a little illustrative anecdote and admonition. The prayer, like the reading, was always in High German—the language of faith in our home—as opposed to the pragmatic, everyday Low German my parents spoke with each other and that we children understood perfectly but were actively discouraged from using ourselves. (Striving to maintain in us a level of comprehension that would allow us to understand what was going on in church, they deliberately and almost exclusively spoke High German to us.) My father's prayer always began with *"Wir danken dir für den Schutz in der Nacht und den heutigen Tag"*—"We thank you for protection through the night and for the [new] day." I heard the rest of the prayer as extemporaneous, but came to realize that, like the opening, it consisted more of rote and ritual than of the "invention" applauded in MB circles—though it was certainly sincere. My father's earnest invocations were undoubtedly a legacy of the prayers he would have heard in his own later childhood, when to speak of safety through the night was surely to allude to manifest perils.

My dad did not grow up in a perfect world, though there must surely have been idyllic strands in his family's collective memory of the several generations of Froeses who, since the late 1700s, had lived in the village of Schöneberg, near the Dnjeper River in Chortitza, the Mennonite Old Colony in what is now Ukraine. His parents had grown up on neighbouring farms facing the village street, side by side. The Froeses and the Falks. His father, my paternal grandfather, had two brothers and seven sisters. The three Froese boys (Grandfather and his brothers), my father told me more than once (though he was never inclined to accompany his telling with any kind of extended commentary), were known among their co-villagers as the capitalist, the evangelist, and the communist. The evangelist was my grandfather, who, while engaged in alternative service around 1909, had been converted to a more lively form of Christian piety than had generally been practised in his home. When he returned to Schöneberg from his forestry duties, he set out to persuade those he held most dear to adopt his new, more vibrant faith. His fiancée was subsequently converted, but rather than expressing the sort of great joy my grandfather had found in his new spirituality, she grew to be dour and irrepressibly pious.

I wasn't yet two when she died, so I have no direct memories of my paternal grandmother. But I remember accounts of her solemn, audible prayers in the presence of all the family at every evening meal—blatant supplications for the soul of her second son, my father's next-younger brother: that he would commit himself to the Lord. Those were uncomfortable moments for my father, and he never forgot them—especially the corrosive impact his mother's tearful entreaties had on his brother, and on himself. His mother's disruptive cajoling would teach him never to expose his own children to that sort of thing. He was prepared to *model*—quietly, consistently, and without commentary—a certain form of Christian devotion, but not to impose it on anyone, least of all his children. I remember asking my dad, when the evangelist Brunk Brothers came to Winnipeg in the late fifties or early sixties, why he was not taking us to the revival campaign (I always liked the music at evangelistic services—a mass choir singing four-part gospel). My father's reply was quick and succinct: "Some preachers make it their business to scare people into heaven," he said. He wasn't interested in exposing us to that.

My father generally didn't tell stories. One of the few anecdotes he could be persuaded to relate was about his leaving his home in the small village of Schöneberg. As the oldest son (then barely seventeen) he was assigned the task of taking the last of the harvest grain to a neighbouring village to be sold—all the while taking care to avoid any suggestion that his family was planning to flee. His father, like other Mennonite lay ministers (including my mother's father, at the same time, in Crimea), had been notified that he was on a list of *Kulaks* destined for exile. So the Froeses set out for Moscow in November 1929, leaving on the table the remnants of their final meal. My dad had memories of waiting, after dark, in a horse-drawn wagon while his parents made one last, hasty, heart-shattering stop at their own parents' homes, to utter their last farewells. When I asked my dad what he remembered as most disruptive about his family's frantic escape to Moscow and beyond during the last weeks in which escape from Stalin's regime was possible, he said it was leaving without the opportunity to say goodbye to his friends, none of whom were allowed any inkling of the fact that he was about to disappear.

What comes to mind now, when I think of that recollection of his, is the poignancy of my father's last days, almost seventy years later, when he was suffering from acute kidney failure. One Sunday morning he asked both his pastor and his attending physician whether he would be committing suicide if he decided not to proceed with dialysis (for which he had been approved and prepared). When each offered a confident no, he agreed to have his dialysis port hastily removed. Then he asked to return to his apartment to have the opportunity to say goodbye to his chums. I accompanied him then, and later in the week found one of his friends—himself a survivor of the Gulag—settled on a couch beside my dad, inspiring each of us with recitations of some of the fine German poetry that had sustained him in hard times.

When I visited my dad alone in the hospital one evening in the final days of his life, I asked him whether there was anything he'd like me to read to him. He answered without hesitation: Psalm 25, which begins, "In you, Lord my God, I put my trust"—a sentiment fully consistent with my father's most prominent sensibilities (which is not to say he never had his own spiritual crises, of which there were hints now and then). I wondered that evening about some of the other themes prominent in that psalm of David, which my father, so avid a Bible reader all his life, must have known intimately. "Do not remember the sins of my youth and my rebellious ways," the Psalmist says; "according to your love remember me" (Ps. 25:7).

I know little about my father's younger days, but realize even now, more and more, how much they must have shaped him. His prevailing memories of his youth prominently featured two related things: corporal discipline at the hand of his father, often prompted by the surveillance of his older sister (he had had two older sisters, and the one closest to him—in both age and sensibility—died when she was ten and he almost nine). His oldest sister, as he recalled, upon returning home after every social gathering of the group of young people who were their mutual friends, would report to their parents every detail of these social encounters. Her accounts of what her younger brother was up to would often result in his being punished for some fairly trivial indiscretion or minor act of defiance.

My father's parents took discipline very seriously, especially when it came to their eldest son. Their home life rested on a scaffolding of strict rules, including those governing how the Sabbath should be spent. More than once I asked my father to recall the Sunday when, as a teenager, he had deliberately ignored his parents' expectation that he spend the afternoon resting in bed ("Remember the Sabbath to keep it holy") and snuck out to join his friends. When he came home later in the afternoon, there were visitors in the house, so nothing was said. His mother gave him a plate of dinner and sent him to bed. But he knew that was not the end of the matter. The next morning he was awoken by his father, who sent him into the orchard to fetch a cherry bough just the right dimensions for a whipping. My father lived well into his eighties and his memories of times like these never faded. There must have been a plethora of stories like this. I heard very few of them, but they surely left their mark on him.

I have no memory of my father holding me on his lap, though he must have done so. I don't recall ever playing an indoor or outdoor game with him, though in the household we played Chinese checkers and crokinole, snakes and ladders and Monopoly. He was a strong swimmer (having spent his childhood near the Dnjeper River), but I don't recall that he ever offered to teach me to swim. I have an innate ability to comprehend things mechanical, and might have learned all kinds of practical skills from his carpenter's hands, but I was never invited to participate in his kind of manual work (though my brothers—ten and eleven years my senior—were). My brothers also had intimate knowledge, I assume—though I don't remember witnessing it—of the piece of harness visibly suspended from a nail on a rafter in the basement of our home, a tool of discipline. In spite of its menacing presence, and threats that made reference to it, that strap of leather was seldom used, if ever. It was never used on me.

Together my father and mother kept the household going through a conventional distribution of work. Mom cooked and baked, cleaned, sewed, and laundered while Dad earned the family's income and minded all things related to finances, the car, the house itself, and—summer and winter—the yard (except for flowers and vegetables, where my mother took charge).

Apart from these divisions of labour they did things together: regularly attending church, visiting with friends and relatives, participating in parent-teacher meetings, and (I can speak here only for myself, but this must have been true for my siblings as well) attending concerts and other events where I, for example, had the opportunity to perform, from figure skating to acting in high school plays.

After breakfast on a weekday my dad would pick up his black tin lunchbox that my mother had packed with a Thermos of coffee, homemade cookies, a piece of fruit, and sandwiches made from her own white bread (she never reneged on the promise she made when she married my dad in 1935, never to let the supply of home-baked bread run out). Every workday was punctuated by his giving my mom, who always accompanied him to the door, a quick kiss before he grabbed his lunchbox and left. In winter, if he was working out-side—as he often had to, roughing houses in the coldest weathers in urban Canada—his sandwiches would freeze before he got to them.

My mom would have dinner ready when he got home—usually a meat-and-potatoes meal, sometimes a hearty homemade soup (cabbage borscht made with beef shanks, or white bean with ham, or carrot and sau-sage: all fabulous) or homemade pasta made into *Verenika* or set out to dry in large sheets on a dough cloth on the kitchen table and then sliced thinly into noodles for chicken noodle soup—with the venerable butcher knife (*Schlachtmassa*) that was otherwise stored deep in the back of a kitchen drawer, its well-honed, stained steel blade tightly wrapped in a cloth.

After dinner my dad would have a bath, and midway through it my mom would quietly leave whatever she was doing and slip into the bathroom to wash his back. Later she might give him a head rub before they retired—always together, without announcement—to their bedroom across the hall from the living room (where any number of us children might still be sitting, doing homework or reading) and held their nightly devotions. They read a passage from Scripture (over the years they read through the Bible from start to finish, over and over again) and knelt by their bed to pray. We might hear the rush of voices from beyond the bedroom door, but nothing was ever said about their nightly ritual. This is simply what they did.

My father's way of thinking about family roles and gender dynamics was surely shaped by his own family background, his religious and ethnic heritage, his particular history as an immigrant denied (unlike his younger brothers) the opportunity to get an education, his class as labourer. Considering where he was "coming from," he might have given expression to significant biases based on gender; he might have suggested, for example, that while it made sense that my older brothers attend university, it was not expected that I would do the same. In fact, neither my mother nor my father gave me any sense that what my brothers were up to wasn't a suitable model for me. My brothers, on the other hand, heading for careers in electrical engineering and medicine/psychiatry, had their own firm opinions, encouraging me (bullying me, if truth be told) while I was in high school to forego studies in the arts in order to get a "real" education, which, in their view, meant skipping history, for example, in favour of physics and chemistry. (Their views reflected little about what they thought women of that day should be allowed to do, but rather spoke to their own chauvinistic ideas about the arts and the sciences.) Interestingly, they were not so far off the mark, as far as I was concerned, as a battery of aptitude tests that placed me firmly in the topmost percentiles for mechanical ability would confirm. When I succumbed to my love of poetry and settled on English literature as a vocation (after flirting seriously with home economics), I continued to enjoy my parents' support (though they had only the faintest notion of what the formal study of English language and literature might entail).

Like any of us, my father occupied a number of social locations and communal affiliations: his nuclear family of wife and five children; his extended family (and my mother's); the neighbourhoods in which he lived as a first-generation Canadian (rural in the beginning, then urban); his MB congregation; his workplaces (as farmer, carpenter, foreman on construction sites, builder). We children saw him through a particular lens. It was only rarely that we were able to observe him from the perspective of his younger brothers, for example, all of whom passed away before I had the insight that would have compelled me to canvass them. They would undoubtedly have had stories to tell.

However, because my father's older sister lived nearby, I *was* able to observe his conflicted relationship with her, rooted in his relentless impatience with her disposition, which had first brought him grief during his teenage years. He resisted, most of all, her seemingly constant tendency to offer stern, often prejudicial, opinions about whatever she heard or saw. My own acute awareness of the never-ending conflict between them kept me from asking her about their early lives together. I had come to see her through his eyes. She lived to be ninety-nine and I could have asked her anything. I regret that I asked her little and realized too late that she clearly had stories of her own.

I knew my father at church, where, when I was very young and unaccountably restless, on one or two occasions he dragged me out of the sanctuary by one ear. I don't recall ever having heard him sing, even though I would have sat or stood beside him many, many times while the congregation sang—in German—any of the great ritual hymns that marked our journey through a Sunday morning. The service invariably began with the *Vorsänger* starting the congregation's *Grosser Gott Wir Loben Dich*, and the monthly Communion service generally included *Zermaltes Brott des Lebens*, a hymn that was always sung at such a droning pace—I found this song particularly affecting because it seemed to allow every member of that predominantly immigrant congregation to channel their lingering trauma and grief. It was well after I left home that my mother (whose singing voice had also eluded me) let me know that my dad had been quite a good singer, and that it was she—my mother, who played the piano by ear—who could not keep a tune.

On rare occasions, my dad would get a call on a Sunday morning inviting him to assist in the service by reading Scripture or praying. He was not a natural performer and it was immediately clear to me that such a request invoked in him a palpable level of stress. Except for these minor, infrequent occurrences, I never heard him speak in public. Church was serious business. We children were all encouraged to attend Sunday mornings, both Sunday school and the congregational service that followed. Going to church was not generally an issue for me, as I recall, though by the time I was about fourteen, I had become increasingly impatient with the texture and quality of Sunday school and announced that I was going to stop attending. My mother, in a weak moment during which she forgot something of the character of her strong-willed youngest daughter, declared then that I had to keep going at least until I was sixteen. I took her at her word: I quit, for good, the Sunday after my sixteenth birthday.

Around that time my parents, who didn't regularly attend Sunday evening church, took it upon themselves one Sunday afternoon, while I was entertaining my best friend at home, to insist that the two of us accompany them to the service that evening. Barely able to believe that they would make such a demand, and so precipitously, I convinced my girlfriend to join me in what one might now think of as "extreme grooming." We applied thick layers of makeup and wildly arranged our hair in such a way as to evoke a certain amount of outrage from those older folks who imagined that frequenting Sunday evening services was a normal thing to do. The evening proceeded without comment. That was the last time my parents made that sort of demand of me.

It was my dad's influence, I think, that compelled them generally to make a deliberate effort to refrain from admonishing or cajoling where church was concerned. My parents, both the children of ministers, knew first-hand that any congregation, from its leaders to its most marginal of adherents, was made up of fallen and fragile individuals. So it was best, my dad would have argued, to mind one's own relationship to the church and its people, to model a modest but consistent piety, and to trust the Good Lord to manage the relationships of each of one's children to God, one another, and the community as a whole.

Of course, I knew my father best as a constant presence in our home. My brothers shared with my dad certain gendered obsessions (cars, for example) and spent summers working construction with him, where they found him firm but fair, exacting but generous. I, on the other hand, had only a rare glimpse into the workday world my father occupied, such as when a fellow academic a generation older than me recalled having worked for my dad as a young man. Recognizing me at an academic conference "as the daughter of your father," he wrote to me spontaneously, generously, several years ago, offering me a rare glimpse of my dad at work. But, more than that, his little anecdote gave me, among other things, an exquisite perspective on what I came to see as my dad's quiet evasion of the straight lines of dogma he had come to see as something of a bluff and a trap. "Your father," this man wrote,

was a skilled finishing carpenter and when he spoke of his trade he used High German; when he spoke of my work he resorted to Low

German. I worked hard to compensate for my lack of talent in the area and he knew it. He knew it well enough not to mention it and only smiled kindly, *leeftolijch* in the extreme, when I pondered his special affection for me.

And so, puzzled by his ways, I asked him how he could be explained. Then he told me something which I will carry with me until my corpus is no more.

He told me the following because he knew I would understand. And I did.

He spoke in High German and with soft authority; he knew, and he understood as he told me that every mile on earth, on average, measures a distance of eight inches difference from beginning of the mile to the end. "*Das muss so sein, weil die Erde rund ist, aber gleichzeitig ist es ein Beweis, dass die Welt rund ist.*"

Then he explained to me that the shortest distance between two points is not a straight line but a curved one and that since he had pondered this into comprehension it had influenced his ways and his work.

Then he showed me the finest of curvatures on the cabinets of his creation...and he smiled with gentle affection.

"Your late father," he concluded, "was a very uncommon Mennonite."

⁂

This commentator's remark about my father's "ways" reminds me that there were rare instances when my dad and I engaged in conversations that verged on the philosophical, about matters of body and soul, for example, or the nature of work. I remember his response when, as a teenager recognizing that individuals might actually have some influence on the world around them, I declared that I would like to become an efficiency expert. He advised me not to go there because, he warned, that role would inevitably make me an outsider to everyone. His (then) young protégé's reference to "the finest of curvatures" of his creation evokes for me my sense of delight at hearing my father explain how it was that he—a poor, landless prairie farmer in the late 1930s—had come to purchase a compact, but handsome and stalwart, oak roll-top desk, which came to represent his private space in the modest house in which I grew up, and which I now own and cherish as one of the lasting, palpable traces of him. He had bought it, he said, simply because it was beautiful. With a well-developed and warm appreciation not only of aesthetic beauty, but also generally of order and structure, this man was always precise and exacting when he worked with his hands. My two male children, who grew up among academics, enjoyed the fact that their Opa was a "worker," and they graciously accepted defeat when, even in his eighties, he challenged them to arm wrestles—and won.

It would be safe to say that my father was present and absent in my life at the same time. He was less a force with whom I actively interacted than the environment, the matrix, in which I grew up. My father was always *there*. Rather than being a companion or mentor, a stern disciplinarian or engaged interlocutor, he was a reliable presence, a sustaining context. He had had two sons and two daughters before I came along and, as far as I can recall, found neither the need nor the occasion to seek any specific, protracted interaction with me, his youngest child. Still, it would never have occurred to me to think of myself as discounted or ignored—even when, in a rare, ironic moment of intimacy, my father confessed matter-of-factly to me that both he and my mother had had a favourite child. Hers had been her oldest son. And his had been my sister, his oldest daughter. Even then I was able to embrace the secure, indubitable consciousness of being unqualifyingly loved and uniquely valued. Even then.

JOURNEY

by **Jean Janzen**

"DOUBLE RAIL"

Winter 1933 and one more mouth
to feed. Seven at home and his schoolroom
full during freeze and thaw. I wonder
what he wanted then as he crossed
the darkening yard where after lessons
he skated with the growing boys. I wonder
what he thought when he entered the warm
kitchen where my mother waited, her apron clean,
dark hair smooth, skin smelling of bread.
What to give a woman when she asks?
Refuge? A thousand years of peace?
Only after the Rapture, he tells my brothers
at the supper table. Premillenialism [sic],
he called it. (And the young child
listens and fears, for who can abide
the day of His coming?)
His broad, immaculate hands butter

the bread, the talk is steady. What difference,
the train stopping at Karkhoff with the Reds
streaming out, or the S.S. blowing bridges
in the spring? Sons. Brothers. Nothing
to stop the flow. A train for escape?
Zug, we called it in German,
as it dragged through the prairie, sighing
into the station with its load.

The congregation stares up at him
in the pulpit. Behind him the words
carved on the wall: "Heaven and earth
shall pass away," as the corn swells
and the lake thickens with fish. In the pews
all of us listening for the Word that speaks
to our feasts and droughts, to the sludgy
bottom of the lake and the silence after harvest.
This life is a journey to another world,
a different glory, he sang out as he stood
shaving at the mirror. He rode the trains
with a carefree spirit, at country crossings
inched the car forward toward the thundering freight
as we gasped and begged. But also, he knew
the shadowy places, the times when life was stopped
and crowded, when he confided, "sometimes I
hardly know who I am." That great distance
and my mother kissing him, so that at the end
he wasn't sure to which home he wanted to go.

October 1970: I arrive by plane from Fresno, California. At the Vancouver airport my niece picks me up to take me to the hospital in Abbotsford. She is a nurse and warns me that my father is dying. His kidneys are shutting down and he may become comatose anytime.

My mother, in her loving concern, has not understood how close he is to death. I have left my husband and three children to take my turn to be with her as Dad declines, not expecting to be the only one out of eight present at this crucial time. But other siblings have made this journey in the weeks before, and I have come now, as he nears his end.

He is tossing and turning. I caress him, this wonderful man, Henry Peter Wiebe, whom I adored all my life, try to calm him, my usually calm parent, with words: "Mom and I are here. It's me, Jean. I have come to be with you." He doesn't acknowledge my presence; he seems lost. I ask the nurses for medicine to soothe my father, and they reply that the doctor has not ordered any. I keep talking, softly, telling him how much I love him; I recite the twenty-third psalm—"Yea, though I walk . . ."—sit silently to allow him sleep, and at last he surrenders, breathes evenly. This could last for hours. When my mother returns from supper, he begins to breathe more slowly, as if now he permits himself to let go. The nurses gather around the bed, standing beside us for the final moment. And then he is gone.

My father's pastor, a kind man, comes to the hospital to pray for my father, and for my mother and me. He thanks God for this man's life of service to his Heavenly Father, for his love to his family and to the church and the world. He will visit us tomorrow. We drive home in the dark, make telephone calls to my siblings, and lay down our weary bodies.

This wild and profound day has finally come to an end. Only this morning I hugged my husband goodbye, back in California—left him to delay his work so that he could take our children to school. And by this evening, my life had changed. My beloved father is dead. And yet I sleep. Then, as first light enters the room, my mother comes in, climbs into my arms, and begins to sob. No words are needed; we comfort each other with our deep sighs. But then she speaks. "I need to tell you about Dad's terrible sadness. About two months ago he awakened me, his body shaking. He had had a terrible nightmare: the recollection of his mother's suicide. Had he ever told her about it? 'Yes, before we married you told me, in case it made a difference to my decision.'" And we both weep, holding each other. Here was a secret that needed to come out. I had lost my father, and now I held his sorrow, which would change my life.

I spend my first five years of life in Saskatchewan, where my father is a country school teacher. My six older siblings are his pupils in the one-room schoolhouse across the yard from our house, known as the teacherage. Its back porch with windows is where I stand and watch the children at play during recess time. In winter when the windows are covered with frost, my mother takes her heated iron and makes a small, arched window for me so I can watch the students at play, my father joining them on the skating rink that he and his older students have made. I watch their circling and falling, hear their muffled shouts, their faces covered with scarves. It is in this porch where my infant brother will lie in a small coffin when I am four. And each winter I hear the clamour of my dad and brothers carrying large tubs of snow into the kitchen behind me where I watch them open a trap door in the floor and dump the snow into a black hole; my mother will pump this water and use it for cooking and washing clothes. At supper we sit around the table, lamp burning in the centre, where we sing a blessing, and Dad folds his hands and thanks God for our food. During this time, when the district does not have money to pay his salary, the government sends dried beans and a large round cheese, my mother clapping her hands in delight as my father lifts it out of the box.

In June of 1939 our family moves to Mountain Lake, Minnesota. After twenty-two years of teaching country school, Dad has been invited to be a part-time pastor in the Evangelical Mennonite Brethren Church. The leap from teaching children to being a pastor is a huge and welcome change to both children and adults, his call based on his reputation as a Bible teacher. Soon, however, he senses a need to be better educated and receives permission to study theology in Minneapolis. He is away from us for most of the week, my older brothers taking care of milking the cow and other duties to free him for this thrill of his lifetime. He travels by bus, and when he comes home, I stand close beside him as he eats his late supper, his clothes smelling of cigarette smoke, listen to his stories about the book of Jeremiah and the joy in his voice, my mother busily serving him. I have missed him.

Three older siblings are thriving in the local high school, the eldest teaching in a country school near the town; soon they are off to college in Kansas. But then Hitler begins to gain power and suddenly we are at war, the draft a threat to my brothers. During that time I am in public school for a year, a kind of relief from the piety of the parochial school. I have loving teachers both in school and in my church Sunday school classes—except for the one who threatens hell if we disobey. Her eyes are black and her hair is pulled back in a black bun. In public school we have a chart and receive a star by our name if we bring scrap metal for the war effort. I point to the pieces of broken farm implements rusting in the pasture between our neighbours and us and ask Dad if I can take some to school for a star. No, he explains, because we do not believe in supporting war. My brothers will ask for ministerial study deferments, and one weekend we visit the camp for Civilian Public Service in Iowa, where handsome young men run their hands over my braids and ask me about school.

Immediately after the war ends, my father resigns from the pastorate to finish his college degree. Three of his children have graduated from Tabor College, and now it is his turn. We move to Kansas, into a house that has become a dormitory for a dozen men. Our family lives on the lower floor. Two of my siblings attend college, my sister is in high school, and my younger brother and I are in grade school. Dad sits at the supper table and talks about his amazing teachers, his pleasure in learning. I also hear his sighs—will he pass genetics, his science requirement? I worry for him. I also worry about my soul's salvation. We drive every Sunday to a house church where he pastors a small flock and offers catechism. I am thirteen and join the class of two to learn what it means to be a baptized member of the church. He is the gentle teacher, my beloved father. Even then I fear for my soul, am sleepless at night, find him at his desk. He shows me the Bible verses that give assurance. I want him to hold me.

Dad pastors three different churches while I am living at home. He is loved as a preacher, counsellor, teacher, and friend. Yet there are the inevitable conflicts—tension between members, varying interpretations of doctrine. Mostly he is private about these troubles, revealing them only in conversation with my mother, but when I am present as a teenage member of the congregation in church business meetings, I see him struggle with tears as he speaks. During these years he is also my Bible teacher at the Academy, and there I witness him as one who is self-assured and playful. I am sorting out my plans for the future, am already dating the man I will marry in a few years. And my father confides in me, in the privacy of our car, "Sometimes I hardly know who I am."

He rarely talks about his family in the Soviet Union. Once or twice I have seen him pull out the passport he used when he moved from Russia to Canada. After his father's early death and then his mother's suicide, his oldest brother immigrates to Canada, a married man with a child, and settles in Saskatchewan. He finds several farmers to agree to pay ship fare for his two teenaged brothers to also come to Canada. They will work for these farmers until the fare is paid off. After the 1905 political disturbances in Russia, the future for landless people was dim, and seemingly open lands waited in Canada. So the two brothers, ages fourteen and fifteen, say tearful goodbyes to their younger, orphaned siblings and depart in the spring of 1910. When they are detained because of eye disease in Liverpool, England, they agree that if the doctor says okay to only one of them, he will take the journey alone. Jake and Henry have rent money for a room, but this delay presses their finances, and so they stand in breadlines with poor English families who kindly claim them as their own. It is my father who gets the okay, and he boards the ship alone—a ride that is bliss for him. He stands on deck, feels the spray wash over him, never suffers from seasickness. When he arrives in Quebec, he takes the train to Dalmeny, Saskatchewan, where he steps off the platform of the station to look for his brother. "Over there, on that field, is your brother, Peter, plowing."

During the 1930s Dad no longer receives news of the siblings he left behind in Russia. Before this, the three brothers in Canada (his second brother had eventually followed him here) had received letters through the two decades since their departure, had heard of the early deaths of two sisters due to tuberculosis and famine. Willie and Daniel have been adopted; sister Susie is a maid to an older couple. Helen has married a widowed man with children. I never hear my dad speak of them. He knows that Ukraine is in turmoil under the rule of Stalin, and that during World War II the only news is devastating news. And he is silent. In 1956 his remaining surviving brother in Canada suddenly receives a letter from the youngest brother, Willie, in Russia: "*Helen, Susie, Marie, und Daniel sind alle gestorben.*" ("Helen, Susie, Marie, and Daniel are all dead.") Willie is the only survivor, now able at last to write after the death of Stalin. My father rarely makes long-distance phone calls, but this time he picks up the phone and calls to tell me the news.

I become a mother in 1957, giving birth to our daughter in a city far from my parents, and in that loneliness I begin to wonder about their childhoods. When they visit I ask about their early years, Dad living in southern Russia, now Ukraine, my mother in Minnesota and Saskatchewan. Mother was the youngest of ten, the darling of the family, as her father broke virgin soil with his sons and led the settlers as pastor of their church. Dad's father also farmed, but because it was his only option. What he loved to do was make music and musical instruments. Dad remembers lying on blankets on the floor of their small house as his father played the violin. He talks, too, about the white, chalk hills outside his former village, how he climbed higher and higher, alone, and wondered if his mother was looking for him. His father was also a lay minister, and he speaks of him as a loving man who would open his long arms wide to invite the congregants to become followers of Jesus. As my father grew older, he made his decision at the invitation of a travelling evangelist, "a Baptist woman who sat behind a table as she spoke." When he arrived in Canada he was befriended by my mother's older brothers, who were training to become teachers and preachers. They saw the potential in my father and encouraged him to go to the "Normal School," the place of training for teachers. In the church my mother saw him in the choir, the most handsome one of all.

My husband, a busy pediatrician, holds a deep desire to travel to Europe, to learn more of its history and visit its art museums. He finds an affordable capital cities tour in connection with a week of meetings in Oxford, England. The original plan is to include Moscow. This is 1966, and my father suggests that his surviving brother in Kazakhstan fly to meet us there and is disappointed when the tour cancels the Moscow stop. In 1975, five years after my father's death, we join another tour of physicians to the Soviet Union—an invitation from the government to visit hospitals and tour the country. But we don't have the courage to contact my cousins after hearing stories of how the KGB allow only a few hours of visiting in some random hotel after relatives have travelled the long distance from Kazakhstan, which became their home after displacement during World War II. But we learn the history, tour Moscow and Kiev, drive out into the Ukrainian countryside among birch forests, and eat borscht and *Verenika*. I see the railroad tracks that carried Dad and his brother out of this country—away from civil unrest and poverty, but also away from their orphaned siblings, the youngest clinging to their legs when they said goodbye, begging and weeping, a story Dad told from the pulpit, his eyes brimming.

Back home in Fresno I create an art book of watercolour paintings and poems to give to my husband, Louis, as a Christmas gift, to thank him for the amazing journey. My nephew, who is a writer, sees the book and tells me that I should continue writing poems, that I should form a writing group that would include him, and we could encourage each other. I gather a small group of writers who meet in my house once a month or so, none of the others writing poems. One of them knows a poet whom she brings along, who tells me that I should go to Fresno State University and study with the poet Peter Everwine. I will eventually also study with the poet Philip Levine. My master's thesis is entitled "Poems about My Father," its centrepiece poem describing the suicide of my grandmother, my father's buried sorrow now laid bare. This is followed by the publication of my first collection, *Words for the Silence*.

‹⁂›

It is July 1989. My husband and I have just arrived in Karaganda, Kazakhstan. A bus full of Mennonite tourists pulls up to a hotel, in front of which stands my cousin, Heinrich, son of Willie. He is with his wife, Valya, who is holding a baby. This is Heinrich, they tell me, father and son both named after my father. The KGB allows us to visit in my cousins' home. From there our bus takes us to Frunze, Kirghizia (Kyrgyzstan), where we visit their father, Willie (my father's brother), and their younger siblings. Cousin Abram has come by train from Siberia to meet us. They embrace us at the door of their home, give me a bouquet of flowers from their garden, and invite us to sit down in their living room, where we sing together "*Grosser Gott, Wir Loben Dich*" ("Great God, We Praise You"), our voices in harmony with the words of this ancient hymn.

‹⁂›

Sometimes when I sit at my desk and wait for the next word, the next line, in a developing poem, I remember observing my father in his joy as he prepared the Sunday sermon. During my high school years he had a small upstairs study where he kept his books, including his beloved commentaries. We all understood that he needed to be solitary and undisturbed, but sometimes he walked down those stairs with the Bible in his hand to announce to my mother that he had discovered something new. While she continued to peel potatoes for lunch, he read the verse or passage with shining eyes and shared his new understanding. And I knew that this was his greatest satisfaction. I also remember the dignity he displayed in the role of pastor, how beautifully he read the rite of marriage from the Common Book of Prayer, how sincerely he offered prayers at the gravesite, and how splendidly he raised his hands in benediction at the end of services.

In January of 1996, after I received a phone call telling me that I had been chosen to receive a major grant from the National Endowment for the Arts, my father came to me in a dream. I was sitting in Christ Church in Oxford, England, singing a hymn. My seat was a carved bench against the wall, under stained-glass windows. My father walked in and sat down beside me. What I remember still is his voice, how beautifully he sang the leap of the octave in the phrase about the Lamb of God. And then I awoke.

THE RELUCTANT FARMER

*by **Maggie Dyck***

I cannot think of any need in childhood as
strong as the need for protection.
—Sigmund Freud

This is a love story. It's about a daughter loving, and being loved by, a father who himself had endured a kind of parental abandonment. Like many a Russian Mennonite saga, my story could be interpreted as a microcosm of the profound transformation that our people experienced, first in Ukraine, then in Canada, during the late nineteenth, and well into the twentieth, century. This transformation—in my case, at any rate—has involved seismic changes in lifestyle without compromising deeply held values. This story is a celebration of those values: generosity, honesty, integrity, unquestioning devotion to family, and a simple, strong faith. This is a happy story.

Where does this happy love story begin? Well, I guess my conception is a good place to start. I was an unplanned but warmly welcomed addition to a family of six: my parents and four siblings. Ours was always a loving and hospitable home. Family came first, but never to the exclusion of friends and relatives from far and near who always seemed drawn to our modest little irrigation farm.

Thirty years have passed since Dad died, but his memory still looms large. My earliest recollection of him goes back to long winter evenings, when I would curl up on his lap in the rocking chair in front of an imposing black and gold ceramic woodstove. He would tell me stories of Russia and sing me Russian folk songs, tears streaming down his cheeks. He loved his adopted Canadian home, but he yearned for the idyllic years he had enjoyed in Crimea, the inviting warmth of the Black Sea, orchards teeming with fruit-laden trees.

My dad, Aron Baerg, was born in 1904 in Fischau (now Rubalovka, Ukraine), a village in the Molotchna Mennonite colony. He was the second of Cornelius and Elizabeth Baerg's seven children. Life had been good to the Mennonites from Prussia who, in the late eighteenth century, had accepted Catherine the Great's invitation to settle in southern Russia, a region that is now Ukraine. Although each family had initially been given a substantial tract of land (approximately 175 acres), that acreage would eventually be insufficient to sustain the rapidly growing Mennonite families. After several generations, the resulting shortage of land forced many of those Mennonite offspring to move, some to so-called daughter colonies, and many farther south to the Crimean Peninsula, a subtropical paradise jutting out into the Black Sea.

So it was that my grandparents and their children, casualties of this land shortage, moved to Crimea to begin a new agrarian life—that is to say, all of their children except Aron, who, at the insistence of his grandparents, remained in Fischau while his parents and siblings moved to their new home far away. It would seem that the grandparents had taken a special liking to this particular grandson, possibly because young Aron was his grandfather's namesake. As traumatizing as this may seem to us now, such familial arrangements were not without precedent in the Russian Mennonite community. Much later, my dad, never bitter about his past, confessed to being distraught at this separation from his immediate family. The distinct advantage to this arrangement, however, lay in the fact that his grandparents were well off. Aron grew up with the finest clothes, he had his doting grandparents all to himself, and he loved riding in his grandparents' handsome *droschke*, an open horse-drawn carriage. And to be sure, his grandmother did take young Aron on rare visits to Crimea so that he could maintain at least a modicum of contact with his parents and siblings. When he was seventeen, his grandmother died; shortly thereafter, his grandfather remarried. The new woman in the Baerg household was apparently not enamoured of her step-grandson, with the result that the young teenager was soon permanently reunited with his family in Crimea. This reunion, welcome though it was, was fraught with sibling rivalry. Not having grown up with them for most of his life, my father hardly knew his brothers and sisters. They in turn resented him for the unusually privileged circumstances in which he had been raised.

This somewhat conflicted chapter in my father's early years surely haunted him to his dying day. The wound of having been "given away" by his parents never entirely healed. As a young child, I recall being puzzled by his occasional assurances that he would never, ever, give me away. Only much later did I come to appreciate the deep hurt that such a comment revealed. But my father was never one to harbour resentment or hold a grudge. Indeed, in later years he and his siblings enjoyed a warm, cordial relationship.

In the 1920s, following the devastation that resulted from World War I and the Bolshevik Revolution, hundreds of Mennonite families from Ukraine decided to migrate to various destinations in the Americas. Among them were my father and his parents and siblings. In April of 1925 they left for Moscow and then Southampton, England, believing they were headed to Mexico, although Canada was their first choice. They were delayed in both cities for several weeks because of Dad's younger sister Tina's eye infection. When several passenger spaces unexpectedly became available on a ship bound for Canada, Dad's parents persuaded twenty-year-old Aron to take his three younger brothers and eight-year-old sister with him on the trans-Atlantic voyage. Their parents and Tina would follow as soon as possible. Imagine the courage it must have taken for my father, only a few years reunited with his family, and still feeling lingering resentment from his siblings, now having this enormous responsibility suddenly thrust upon him. But they survived the voyage and arrived safely in Rosthern, Saskatchewan, that spring. They were welcomed by local Mennonite families who took them in, but who in turn expected the boys to help on the farms.

The rest of the family arrived some months later, in the fall of 1925. Once more reunited, the family moved to Crowfoot, Alberta. There was a Mennonite Brethren.(MB) church in nearby Namaka, which is where Dad met and married my mom, Gertrude Willms, in March of 1928. The young couple settled on a farm purchased from the Canadian Pacific Railway. The first few years were good ones. But then the Great Depression struck, followed by a number of years of drought, dust storms, and crop failures. The hardships that followed resulted in my grandparents and most of Dad's siblings moving to Ontario. But Dad, his young bride, and a brother and sister stayed in Alberta. Although the Depression was difficult, my parents never complained, their only regret being that there was never enough money left over to give to the church's mission projects.

My siblings were born in Crowfoot, but because of the lack of good schools, my parents decided to move the family a hundred miles south, to Coaldale. Not only were the schools much better in this considerably larger community, but it also had a vibrant MB congregation. It was there that I made my appearance, the last in a family of five children. My siblings were all considerably older, so I was the family pet, a role I came to relish. My eldest brother left home to attend college in Winnipeg when I was only five, so my recollections of him in those early years are vague. I recall my other siblings pampering me more than my parents did; when they too left to continue their education I was sorry to see them go. Not only did I miss their company, but I was now also expected to do many of their chores on the farm.

I spent a lot of time with my father on this modest farm in southern Alberta. Ours was a relatively small venture, an irrigation farm of eighty acres, three miles from town. It was truly a mixed operation, a combination of crops and livestock. In the latter category, we had a little bit of everything: cows, horses, pigs, sheep, geese, ducks, chickens, and of course the requisite cats and dogs. I loved all the animals, and often, in the wintertime, ducklings or chicks or even little piglets were brought in from the cold barn to warm up in a box behind the kitchen stove. Dad was hugely amused by his little five-year-old girl dressing the piglets in doll clothes and taking them for a stroll in a doll carriage; eventually they would either wriggle out of the clothes or soil them as only piglets can. In addition to looking after our domesticated menagerie, my father wrested from our small acreage annual crops of wheat, barley, oats, alfalfa, and, above all, sugar beets. Those sugar beets proved to be the bane of my teenage years. An early champion of gender equality, my father expected me to work as hard during harvest time as my brothers had when they were still at home. This meant hoeing for a couple of hours in the morning before catching the school bus. Harvesting those infernal beets also often involved late evenings. Many a night I stood on the beet topper, watching the conveyor belt as the sugar beets—as well as dirt and stones—pelted down on my frozen hands. Because of the beet harvest, I missed a lot of school, one year in particular, my prowess in algebra suffering accordingly.

Dad assumed that everyone would pitch in and help, but he was always gentle, never domineering. When Mom suggested to him that perhaps my back was not strong enough to lift heavy bales of straw, Dad immediately relented and reassigned me to driving the tractor, a decidedly easier task and one I enjoyed to no end. And so it went from year to year. We made do with very little, yet never felt impoverished. Although Dad took farming seriously enough, he was never very good at it. For him it was merely a means to an end, providing for his family and making it possible for his children to pursue an education.

Indeed, education was of paramount importance to my parents, second only to their faith. They struggled valiantly to be able to send all five of us to Mennonite Brethren Bible College (MBBC) in Winnipeg. A combination of astonishing frugality and ingenuity in raising badly needed cash made this possible. For example, the year one of my brothers was about to leave for college in Winnipeg, there simply weren't any extra funds to pay for his bus fare. In anticipation of my typing classes in high school that fall, Dad had purchased a typewriter. Well, at the last minute the typewriter was sold and my brother was off to pursue his dreams. Meanwhile, I was quite capable of curbing my disappointment, not being even remotely interested in anything that might prepare me for a job as a secretary!

A regular source of supplementary income was our periodic chicken slaughter. On a Friday after school, Dad and I would catch twenty to forty chickens. He would kill them, then we would plunge them into boiling water, loosening the feathers for plucking. I remember the pungent smell of those damp feathers to this very day. Next came the eviscerating part of the process, a task at which I soon became an unwilling expert. But this onerous chore was made somewhat more palatable by the prospect of taking the newly plucked and eviscerated poultry to Lethbridge, where Dad and I would sell them door to door. Awash in cash, we would head off to the grocery store, where the fruits of our labour always included a snack of fresh cinnamon buns, a ring of sausage, and a bottle of Orange Crush. All was well in my little world!

We were constantly encouraged to read. I devoured all the Nancy Drew books, and I adored *Anne of Green Gables*. My siblings and I took great pride in being the first Mennonite family in our community to own a complete *Encyclopedia Britannica* set. How well I remember the handsome wooden case in which these volumes were stored. And for as long as I can remember, we subscribed to the *National Geographic* magazine. The glossy full-colour photos of exotic people and places fired my imagination, and I dreamt of future adventures in these far-flung lands. Mind you, I was frustrated by my father's somewhat puritanical instincts. As soon as each issue arrived, he would carefully inspect it for any photos of bare-breasted African or South American women. Very meticulously, he covered the offending images with Band-Aids, leaving me to speculate as to what unspeakable lewdness I had just been protected from.

Both of my parents had planned to pursue their educational goals, only to have those dreams dashed by World War I, the Bolshevik Revolution, and then their precipitous migration to Canada. What's more, the Coaldale MB church frowned on so-called higher education. One of our ministers put it this way in his crude German: "*Unsere Prediger kommen von hinter die Kuh*" ("Our preachers come from behind the cow"). In this anti-intellectual environment, my parents' continued insistence on the value of education constituted a real act of courage. There's little doubt in my mind that Dad's interest in education and learning was piqued by his two college professor brothers-in-law. Supporting the educators in Coaldale's private Mennonite schools—a high school as well as a Bible school—was very important to Dad, who served as chairman of the Bible school board for fourteen years. But his commitment to education also found a practical application. Every Friday, he and I would make the rounds to the homes of all the teachers in these schools, delivering to each one hampers of fresh eggs, a freshly slaughtered chicken, cream, and milk. His quiet generosity was much appreciated by the teachers, who were paid very little. Many of these grateful families became lifelong friends.

Music was an integral part of our household, and it was Dad who encouraged our music making. What wonderful times we had, gathered around the piano. My sister was the pianist, and my brothers did their best with the guitar, clarinet, and trumpet while Dad played the mandolin. I sang, as did Mom, her ubiquitous knitting needles clacking away. The cacophony resulting from this unconventional ensemble was truly Schoenbergian, but we loved every minute of it. We all took music lessons despite our limited financial resources. Bill, the trumpeter, practised his noisy instrument outdoors where our three dogs would accompany him with their howling. Dad's encouragement resulted in two of my brothers becoming music professors in Mennonite colleges. I married a conductor and have been actively involved in music all my life. For Dad this was surely a vicarious way of living his dream through his children. He had always wanted to study music. In Ukraine as a very young man he had briefly conducted a choir. I often wonder what went through his mind years later as he sang those mournful Russian folk songs to me. What might have been had world events and family circumstances not cruelly cut short whatever modest musical ambitions he harboured?

The life of our community revolved around the church. Our family participated fully, attending all the many Sunday and mid-week services and of course singing in various choirs. Dad was a respected deacon for a number of years, although he was, for a brief time, not allowed to assist in the serving of Communion after certain "liberal transgressions" occurred at my sister's wedding. She had had the temerity to move the church organ from the centre of the sanctuary off to the side in order to facilitate the bridal procession. Such brief "shunnings" were the absurdities one could expect in a provincial, parochial environment. But they did nothing to disrupt our continuing participation in the life of the church.

The church services themselves were long—very long—and, for the most part, unrelentingly boring. One senior minister in particular would indulge regularly in German prayers lasting at least ten minutes, and what's more, by the time the two-hour service started, we had already had an hour of Sunday school. The men and women sat on opposite sides of the sanctuary, the young boys and girls in front. My friends and I speculated about the reason for this gender separation and came to the conclusion that it had to do with the monthly Communion, which always concluded with the "brotherly kiss." To have men and women kissing each other was simply unthinkable.

The church had codes of behaviour to which especially the young people were expected to conform. Whispering in church, for example, was strictly "verboten," although it happened not infrequently. On one occasion, when I was caught whispering yet again, the presiding minister not only reprimanded me from the pulpit, but then also asked my father (a deacon!) to come and get me and have me sit with him. I can only imagine how humiliated my dad must have been to get up from his seat, walk to the front of this big church, cross over to the women's side, take me by the hand, and lead me back to sit with him among all the men. But then he did a most wonderful thing, something I shall always remember: he put his big, protective arm around me for the rest of the service. Later, at home, not a word was ever said about the incident. Perhaps the silent treatment was punishment enough—well, perhaps, but to this day I believe Dad was signalling to me that I wasn't guilty of anything particularly reprehensible.

At home, our spiritual nurture was left mostly to my mother. Topping that agenda was seeing to it that all of us were "saved," "converted," "born again"—use whatever term you wish. This was of utmost importance, ostensibly sparing us from going to hell when we died. I was terrified of hell, and so, as extra "fire insurance," I got "saved" numerous times in the privacy of my bedroom. If that sounds somewhat cynical, let me also say that I deeply appreciated Mom and Dad's simple, unquestioning faith. They were devout believers. Nothing was more important to them than that we embraced their faith and made it ours. Every morning at breakfast we would read a page from the *abreiss Kalendar* (a calendar of daily devotionals) and Dad would read a passage from Scripture and lead us in prayer. Mom and Dad's social interactions with their friends sometimes included a devotional time as well. When I was quite young, I would occasionally sit in with all of them. When it came time to pray, we all got down on our knees and each of us was expected to pray. Mostly I feigned sleep when it came my turn.

Then there was the matter of baptism. At some point in our teens it was expected that we would be baptized. I was most unenthusiastic about this rite of passage, but the pressure to conform was intense. Most of my girl-friends were baptized when they were in their mid-teens. So, one evening, at the age of fifteen, I went to Dad, who was working in the garden, and said, "Dad, I think I should get baptized." He was quiet for a moment, and then he asked, "Do you want to get baptized?" I said, "No, not particularly," and his immediate response was, "Then don't do it. You should be baptized only if and when you want to." This from a deacon in the church for whom the baptism of his youngest daughter would surely have been a badge of honour. I was so relieved by his unexpected response that I gave him a big kiss and ran away happily. However, I was old enough to know that I was only postponing the inevitable; in order to be eligible to attend any MB post-secondary school, I would have to be baptized.

And so, at the age of eighteen, I announced my intention to be baptized. What a harrowing process! First there was the testimony each baptismal candidate had to give to the entire congregation. This always included a declaration of your faith and, most importantly, the specific date you had been saved. After your presentation—and occasionally some cross-examination—you were sent to the church basement while the congregation decided your fate. To my great relief, I was accepted. But in my case there was one more hurdle to clear. One evening, two deacons came to our farmyard and invited me to get in their car with them. There I was reprimanded for having sung in the church choir while wearing sleeves that were too short. To qualify for baptism and church membership, I would have to, then and there, pray for forgiveness. I began to pray in English, but the Coaldale MB God was apparently a German-speaking deity, so I was asked by the deacons to pray in German. Having struggled through a suitably contrite "*auf Deutsch*" prayer in this car-turned-confessional, I was now deemed fit to be baptized.

The baptismal service itself was a nightmare. Baptism in the MB Church is by immersion, and in those days it was conducted outdoors. Fortunately, we had a pond near the church, but it was early June and the water was cold. There we girls were, lined up, knee deep in water, trying to keep our dresses down, awaiting our turn to be submerged, all the while keeping a wary eye out for the water snakes that had little appreciation for this ecclesiastical incursion into their territory. I found it exceedingly difficult to concentrate on the spiritual import of the occasion! After we had retreated to the shed that served as a dressing room, we were so giddy that our laughter threatened to disrupt the remainder of the baptism. Next, sporting heads of wet hair, we made our way into the church, where we were officially accepted as members and allowed to participate in our first Communion. For Dad, to serve his youngest child her first Communion was a shining moment of faith, culminating a spiritual journey he and I had travelled together. As embarrassing as I found the whole baptism experience to be, I was nevertheless pleased by the obvious satisfaction it gave to Dad.

Any recollection of my experiences with my father would be incomplete without reference to his *joie de vivre,* his sheer pleasure in living. Dad had a playful, fun-loving side to him that I found utterly delightful. He built a huge swing and a volleyball court in our large treed yard. He even outfitted the volleyball court with electric lights for evening games, an innovation frowned on by the church elders. He enjoyed immensely the young people who frequented our place. There were also wonderful family picnics, often coinciding with blueberry-picking expeditions. And in the winter there were games: Chinese checkers, dominoes, snakes and ladders. Dad was always a keen and competitive participant. But as much as he enjoyed group activities, I always felt that it was the one-on-one relationships he relished most of all. One of his special pleasures was having me comb and fuss with his hair. Sometimes I would put little ribbons or clips in it, always resulting in great levity. And then there was watching sitcoms on television! Dad's favourite TV show was *I Love Lucy.* This was a regular and much-anticipated highlight. The MBs didn't allow television in those days, so we went to our General Conference Mennonite relatives who had one. I've never seen Dad laugh, tears streaming down his cheeks, the way he did watching that show. And I would laugh with him, savouring those shared moments of pure, uncomplicated joy.

When I graduated from high school, I followed my siblings' example and left home to further my education. By this time Mom and Dad were relieved that their parenting days were finally over. My first choice was to go to university, but that was not an option as far as my parents were concerned; they felt I was too young for such a secular environment. They assumed I would go to MBBC, in Winnipeg. That's where my siblings had gone, and, what's more, my uncle, J.A. Toews, was the president of the college. So that was the end of it; I headed off to Winnipeg and was quite happy to do so. My brothers and sister had all found their spouses there, but I was determined to break that pattern. It was not to be. I met Howard Dyck, a student from Winkler, and because of our mutual musical interests, we were immediately and powerfully attracted to each other and quickly fell in love. My parents, happy to see their youngest child on her way, gladly accepted Howard as a prospective son-in-law.

The summer we were married, Howard arrived in Coaldale a week before our wedding to help with the actual preparations. That's when I experienced Dad's irrepressible sense of humour in a new and unexpected way. A couple of days before the wedding, Howard was given an assignment that would prove whether or not he was worthy of this young woman's hand in marriage. The farm, as I've mentioned before, was a hand-to-mouth operation, so we needed to raise a little extra cash for food to feed the 450 or so wedding guests. Dad and his young son-in-law-to-be headed to the pasture where the sheep were grazing. Pointing to a suitably plump specimen, Dad said, "Howard, get me that sheep!" The sheep, sensing its impending doom, fled, with Howard in hot pursuit. Eventually, having bravely wrestled the animal to the ground, Howard tied its legs and hoisted it into the trunk of the car. Meanwhile, Dad was bent over, roaring with laughter! As for the poor sheep, it defended itself inelegantly as only a cornered sheep can, in anticipation of which Dad had lined the car trunk with a protective layer of cardboard. After delivering the sacrificial sheep to the stockyards and collecting the money, Dad and Howard removed the soiled cardboard and replaced it with clean newspaper. Then, off to the bakery to collect a trunkful of freshly baked buns for the wedding reception. The wedding itself was an unqualified success, and the marriage "took." Fifty-three years later we are still deeply in love.

Two years after my wedding, Mom and Dad sold the farm and moved to southern Ontario to be near two of their children and their families. Howard and I and our children also moved to Ontario a few years later, so Mom and Dad could now enjoy many of their grandchildren on a regular basis. Leaving the farm was a huge relief for Dad. He had always been a reluctant farmer. He and Mom enjoyed their last twenty years in St. Catharines, where the climate was relatively temperate and the fruit was plentiful, just as it had been in Crimea. But amid these autumnal pleasures, there were also lingering dark memories of those early tumultuous years in Ukraine. These came to the fore when I was anticipating a trip to Soviet Russia in 1983. Because of my parents having been born in what would become the Soviet Union, Dad was convinced the authorities would not allow me to leave Russia. When it became clear that I was determined to go, Dad prayed a long, impassioned prayer on my behalf. His prayer was answered and I returned safely to Canada.

So who was Aron Baerg really—this unassuming, uncomplicated man? I remember him primarily for his generosity. He had little money, but anything that he could grow or raise on the farm was gladly and quietly shared with others. He was a man of few words; he was defined more by what he did than by anything he said. He was protective, especially of his family, and most especially of his daughters. Those instincts—although I mostly appreciated them—annoyed me when it came to dating. In this regard, my brothers weren't monitored nearly as closely as I was. Perhaps Dad thought I was still that little girl curled up on his lap, needing protection. Much later, I often wished it were so. Dad rarely got angry, although I do recall two specific incidents when he did. As a ten-year-old, I remember feeding coal to the pigs because I loved the crunching sound they made when they ate it. My father was not amused by this; his insights into the nutritional requirements of swine were clearly beyond my ken. I was duly contrite at having caused potential harm to my animal friends. On another occasion I put a recent discovery of mine into action. I had learned that it was possible to put chickens to sleep by simply tucking their heads under their wings. Their primal response to darkness was to nod off almost immediately. This experiment, too, met with Dad's disapproval. When he came home, he couldn't navigate the driveway because of all the slumbering fowl blocking his way. But in my experience, those two minor episodes constituted the extent of his anger toward me.

There are psychologists who suggest that daughters get along better with their fathers than with their mothers, and sons better with their mothers than with their fathers. I don't think our situation could be categorized that neatly. When I think back to what Dad gave me, I would say his greatest gift to me was his love and respect for my mother. Indeed, it was that which nurtured me, drawing me close to both of my parents. Theirs was a traditional relationship. Mom looked after the house and garden, while Dad's baili-wick was the livestock and crops. The two of them discussed finances and church-related matters seated at the kitchen table or on the big swing out in the garden. But Mom was nothing if not opinionated, and for the most part, Dad deferred to her pronouncements. From time to time, however, when he had had enough, he would quietly but firmly say "Truda," and she knew she had overstepped the bounds. Often, after having delivered herself of yet another polarizing political viewpoint, she would turn to Dad and say, "*Na Papa, sag du das letzte Wort*" ("Well, Dad, why don't you have the last word?"). Rarely was his last word a dissenting one. I grew up believing that it was normal for all women and girls to be individuals and to say what they thought. I assumed their opinions were to be taken seriously.

The grandchildren of Opa Baerg remember a playful, sweet man who loved nothing better than to take them for walks to the nearby Welland Canal to watch foreign freighters come through the locks. Invariably there were also little treats of candy and frequent trips to the Avondale Dairy Bar for ice cream. It was telling that, at his funeral, each of his grandchildren was convinced that he or she had been his favourite. My youngest son, who was quite young when Dad died, missed his Opa's big hands, which would completely envelop his small ones, making him feel secure and loved. I am grateful that my children experienced my father, their grandfather, the very same way I did.

In the end, all I can say is that this gentle, strong giant was a good man and a wonderful father. He and I loved each other very much, and I miss him every day.

MY FATHER AND
THE PIETIES

*by **Raylene Hinz-Penner***

I treasure one of the earliest photos I have of my father: a young dairy farmer is flanked by his two-year-old daughter in a ruffled dress and his tamest cow in a sandy cow lot in the southwest corner of Kansas in 1952. My father is holding my hand, positioned between me and a Guernsey cow, his knee protectively leaned forward as a barrier between me and the world. Mama sees that my shoes are freshly polished, my hair is combed, and I am dressed to go to town with my father for an errand; she knows he will set me on the counter and ask me to speak to the clerk as he pays his bill.

Flash forward a few years. It is a Sunday in the late 1950s, and I am in the back seat of our wide-grille mint-green Mercury with my younger sister. We are in the parking lot of the little Jack and Jill grocery on the south edge of town, having come into town after driving the fifteen miles into the Oklahoma Panhandle to attend the morning worship service at Friedensfeld Mennonite, a small, white-framed church set in the corner of a pasture. We have taken this extra time to drive in to nearby Liberal before we return to our farm east of town for our regular Sunday dinner—roast beef, carrots and potatoes, *Zwiebach*, and homemade pie—because my father must have the Sunday edition of the *Daily Oklahoman*. I watch with pride as he unfolds his long legs and straightens himself into a military bearing to walk briskly into the grocery in his black suit, white shirt, and tie. He returns almost instantly with the thick Sunday edition of the newspaper, still laughing and calling back over his shoulder to the clerk or another customer.

Before he opens the car door, he leans through the open window and tosses onto my mother's lap a sack of peanut clusters and a sack of maple nut goodies, two of his favourite candies, for Sunday-afternoon snacking. "Here you go, Kitty," he smiles, using his pet name for my mother. My heart bursts with pride that this man is my father.

My childhood years in the Bible belt were not the kindest time for a Midwestern girl with aspirations, the first-born of two daughters. Maybe that is why I modelled myself after my father, rather than after my small and demure, pretty and modest, but retiring mother. I noticed my father's community status, his larger-than-life persona that filled a room. I was named for my father; Mama had found the name "Raylene" carved into a café counter in central Oklahoma while she was pregnant with me before they moved to the farm east of Liberal, where they had agreed to restore a half section of land left to coyote hunters after the Dust Bowl disaster had covered it with sand. Mama had pounced on the name she gave me because my father's middle name was Ray.

Like my father I was outgoing, outspoken, even brash sometimes, and argumentative—qualities cultivated in the 1950s more in boys than in girls. And, of course, I could see who had the power of decision making in the larger world, though my parents worked and made decisions together. My father was larger than life, filled a room with his stories, his laughter, even his stature—six feet two, and over two hundred pounds, my daddy loved to eat with the same kind of gusto with which he lived the rest of his life. He had long arms and legs, had played basketball and baseball in high school, and exuded the confidence of an athlete. I was tall for a girl, big-boned and strong, having attained my adult height by age twelve. I knew "demure" would never fit me.

Indeed, it was not only my father's extroverted personality that I loved, but also his approach to religion and discipleship, somehow different from that of other Mennonite fathers I knew. Though he was strict, my father somehow never really seemed bound by piety. I do not refer here to the conventional sense of the term, as in "being religious or reverent," but rather piety as that quality of holding beliefs "with unthinking conventional reverence." Daddy possessed a slightly irreverent sense of humour, could let slip a mild vulgarity (though he did *not* take the Lord's name in vain), and he overate; in fact, he did very little in moderation in his life. Good thing he didn't drink. His effusive love of life extended to the people he encountered both in church and on the street. He seemed to me to have a very real need to get the rest of the world to "lighten up" and enjoy life, overcome their quotidian anxieties, and laugh. Furthermore, he seemed not to be particularly rule-bound or cowed by the need for veneration; Daddy was downright disgusted with sanctimoniousness, but a keen admirer of dignity. Thus, that complicated issue of pride with which so many Mennonites seemed to struggle was seemingly not an issue for Daddy, who believed in the innate worth of all individuals and never allowed anyone in our household to "put herself down."

Looking back now, I want to attribute my father's *joie de vivre* to some vestige of Lutheranism he still harboured deep in his being, assuming that we "typical" Mennonites come with a bit of dour victimhood, a bit of a martyr's complex. My father was never a practising Lutheran, and I didn't know until after he was gone that my father's people had been Lutherans in the "old country." Daddy's great-grandparents were Lutherans born near Gdansk, according to an old family Bible. They came to the United States among the few Lutherans aboard the *Teutonia* bound from Hamburg in 1874. I don't believe Daddy knew about these great-grandparents; none of his siblings knew of them when I researched the genealogy. No one in his family cared about genealogy or the past; they were desperate to make good lives for themselves in the present. Daddy's great-grandparents, Christoph and Johanna Freitag Hinz, in their forties when they arrived, first homesteaded in central Kansas along what is still known today as Dutch Avenue, running west out of Hesston. They joined the Hoffnungsau Mennonite Church near Buhler—I always suspected this might have been because it was easier to get land from the railroad alongside the mass of Mennonites with whom they came. They lived in Kansas until they died. Their children moved on to Corn, Oklahoma, where the last of his siblings still live.

When I learned of the family's Lutheran past, I remembered a childhood event. My father returned late one afternoon, bubbling and full of stories after attending the memorial service of a Lutheran neighbour. Apparently, after the service, he had somehow found himself involved in a theological discussion with the Lutheran priest who had conducted the service. Daddy described the priest as seated in his robe with his leg slung over the armchair in his office, having a cigarette and a glass of wine—for me, a startling image of a man of God. Daddy exuberantly described their conversation; even as a child I sensed that for some reason my father had found this conversation intriguing, even liberating. Why did Daddy tell us about this encounter? Why do I remember it?

Recently I read a description of Martin Luther's marriage to a former nun, which he decided would "please the father, rile the pope, cause the angels to laugh and the devil to weep."* There was a bit of that flavour to my father's values and lifestyle. Though he never referred to the notion of sinning boldly, because my father did nothing timidly, I would guess that he also sinned boldly. We are led to believe that Luther's home with his wife, the nun Katharina von Bora, and their six children was lively and happy: they bowled on the lawn, made music and sang, hosted friends for dinner. That sounds very much like my father's family of seven children who teased each other and laughed at the world; imitated each other and made faces to entertain one another; sang hymns around the piano, which they played by ear since there was no money for lessons; stayed up late at night laughing and arguing raucously; raised their voices to frightening levels, according to my mother—just because they could not give up the day.

Though I grew up Mennonite, studied catechism, and joined our conservative little rural General Conference Mennonite Church as a teenager, though I understood the pieties necessary for a young Mennonite girl growing up in the 1950s—no drinking, no dancing, no swearing, no sexual transgressions—I also always understood that those pieties weren't necessarily my saving grace. I wonder whether my daddy's Lutheran roots had somehow settled deeply in his soul, loosened him up, given him the confidence that though he might mouth the words (and he loved memorization

---

* "Katharina von Bora (1499–1552)," Welcome to LutherCountry, n.d., accessed July 4, 2018, https://www.visit-luther.com/reformation-heroes/katharina-von-bora.

of poems and Bible verses and taught Sunday school all his days), he didn't really believe in original sin or hell, at least not enough to emphasize them. When a wave of child evangelism swept through our church, my father's mouth curled in derision at the thought of it, which must have seemed to him like scaring children into heaven.

Daddy was big on reason and free will. When our high school youth group questioned the virgin birth, we were not hushed. An older woman in our church threw a fit and damned our doubts. My daddy and some other church fathers organized a Sunday-afternoon discussion on the topic, and the irate church matriarch was allowed to speak her mind in witness to us, but we doubters were also allowed to voice our questions. I don't remember any resolution of the issue then, or ever in my own thinking, but the lesson that stuck with me was that faith is a wrestling match, probably throughout one's existence, and reasonable theological questions, even doubts, are to be honoured. Ambiguity is a way of life for such a believer—certainly for the English professor and literary critic that I would become in my professional life.

I think about the way my father taught Sunday school. I was privy to his reviews of what had happened in his Sunday school class as we drove the fifteen minutes home from church each week. Daddy shared with his wife and daughters what he had learned from leading the discussion: he detailed Sylvia's doubts or fears; he smiled over Jim's heretical questions. Always, the Sunday school texts were applied to complicated, real-life situations: How do you live this out? What does this mean for communal life? A driver who did not necessarily mind the speed limit, Daddy was always jovial and talkative after church as he sped down the highway, responding to the sermon, asking us what we thought, listening carefully, perhaps pushing back on our interpretations. Church was a social event that energized my father.

Furthermore, Daddy never seemed to me to be quite on board with that Mennonite injunction that we must be "in the world but not of the world." I had never been to a dance at my high school, but when I was selected as a candidate for the homecoming royalty, my parents bought me a beautiful cobalt blue suit from the best store in Liberal (I felt guilty for the expense), and they were there among the crowd of parents watching the first dance. On the other hand, I was never allowed to go out on a Saturday-night date until I had studied my Sunday school lesson. Devotion and reverence (how we sat in church, even our posture) were very important to my father. When I was taller than anyone else at age twelve, and certainly taller than all of the boys my age, I began to feel self-conscious, to slump, round my shoulders, try to disappear. Daddy threatened to build a crosspiece out of wood and rope it against my back if I didn't stand up straight! I knew he wouldn't actually do such a thing, of course, but the image of my shoulders roped to the crosspiece improved my posture dramatically.

My father, who had served in the US military during the waning years of World War II, always carried himself with pride, dignity, and a military bearing, and I thought of him as somehow different from other fathers in our church. I am certain that few others in that little Oklahoma Panhandle congregation had a military history. The family into which my father was born the fifth of seven children, and the third son, suffered economic failure during the Depression, which had necessitated their moving off the farm into the small town of Corn, Oklahoma. They were barely eking out a living when Daddy's father died suddenly at age forty-seven, leaving the family destitute. The oldest son still at home, Daddy took over his father's truck-driving job as a seventeen-year-old senior in high school. Upon graduation from high school, and heeding the advice of his uncles who noted that there were no jobs locally during the war, he joined the US Army as a noncombatant to support his mother and two younger siblings.

Other Oklahoma Mennonites also forsook their pacifism to stand against Hitler during those years, and the US Army became the vehicle for the little post–high school education my father received. Daddy had grown up speaking High German, and the army needed those language skills as the war was coming to an end. He was sent to Germany's oldest university, in Heidelberg, to brush up on the German vernacular, so that he might serve as an interpreter to help interrogate German prisoners following liberation, as the United States tried to find members of Hitler's ss.

My father fell in love with Heidelberg, European cathedrals, and the liturgy of high church. He was, it seemed to me, a strange and wonderful mixture of classical interests like the song "Ave Maria" and the common man's more simple interests. For example, I will never forget the evening he came in from the dairy barn and, while changing out of the striped overalls he wore for milking the cows, overheard the strains of some classical orchestra we were playing from our limited collection of old vinyl albums. In his long underwear and socks, no doubt still smelling of the dairy barn, Daddy laughingly danced his own elegant imitation of the ballet maestro Rudolf Nureyev. Arms straight out as if flying, pirouetting on one leg, gracefully relying on the balance he must have developed as an athlete, Daddy danced before the red glow of our living room stove. Mama, my sister, and I laughed and cheered. Obviously, my father was not particularly modest; comfortable in his own skin, he transmitted a natural ease with the physical body that helped his daughters to feel likewise about their own.

On Valentine's Day, Daddy would bring home from town a big red heart-shaped box of chocolates for my mother and smaller versions for my sister and me. When he bought Mama a nightie for Christmas, he might buy my sister and me smaller, more girlish versions. Today, I see that these simple gifts were ways in which Daddy affirmed us—bodies, minds, and souls. His gifts were lavish for a dairy farmer's earnings, and with my mother's expertise as a seamstress, we felt well dressed, proud of our appearance. Before church on Sunday mornings Daddy noticed our clothing, twirled us around to comment on our hair (or maybe chide us on the length of our skirts during the miniskirt days). I remember sitting at our family table as a college girl come home to report to her family on a life I knew they all envied. My fingernails were painted a deep scarlet and Daddy took my hands into his and remarked, "Wow, that is dark nail polish." Maybe I wanted him to notice that I had quit biting my nails, a habit of mine he had abhorred. He carefully put my hands back down on the table and said, "Actually, it looks nice."

My formative years in the 1950s still honoured the old mantra that children were to be seen and not heard. Yet, because my father, along with my Oklahoma uncles, were great storytellers, I always wanted to hang out in the room where they held forth with their hilarious retellings of their experiences, no doubt embellished for effect. I distinctly remember the time Daddy turned to me while I was still an adolescent in just such a setting and said, "Raylene, tell them about...." That endorsement, the right to tell a story, his confidence in my abilities to hold forth in this circle, to actually pull it off, would make a huge difference in my self-confidence as a public speaker.

Privately, Daddy's stories were also for instruction; I am reminded of his lesson in response to my hot-tempered displays of anger. More than once during my adolescence my father told me the story of his aunt. As a young woman in a fit of rage, she had made a public spectacle of herself for the whole town of Corn to see when she had kicked over the fifty-gallon gas drums at the Main Street service station. Daddy described her almost demonic possession as she sent the large oil drums thundering down the street. Though Daddy intended this as a lesson to me about uncontrolled rage, secretly I was caught in my own imagination of the scene, of her amazing courage and showmanship. Unfortunately, my father's aunt had grown into middle age only to lead a heartbreaking life of mental illness. Daddy warned that temper flares, that lack of self-control had been the curse of her youth; I needed to get hold of myself.

Surely my definition of positive masculinity was formed by watching my father's model, even gauging how far I could go on the scale of androgyny. Over time, I recognized that I was not petite or cute or girlish; however, my own more boyish style did not diminish my self-concept. Though it would have been nice to have had a son to help him on the farm, my father never even hinted that one of his daughters should have been a boy. He and our mother went to the dairy barn together for each milking, and we girls drove the tractor and helped with the dairy when we were needed. My sister and I took immense pride in the "boys' work" that we could do just as well as any boy. No strict demarcation between girls' and boys' work was enforced in our household.

Daddy had in earlier years reduced the number of acres he chose to farm; family life was too important to him to spend all of his hours farming, no matter the money. Our work on the farm, though always secondary to our "jobs" to educate ourselves as young women, seemed to be a source of pride for our father. In fact, I grew up believing that my father had an explicit preference for girls. He once said to me longingly, "I wish you could have met my mother." I watched his special love for and admiration of his sisters when their family was together. He certainly believed that girls should vie with boys for top academic honours. In high school my chief competition for top of the class was a boy named Harold. My father believed my test scores should always exceed Harold's, even in math, where girls were often given a pass since boys were believed to be innately better at math and science (as it turned out, I actually needed a pass in math!). In those years it seemed to me that too often I found my father sitting at the dining room table, wanting to go outside and do chores but waiting until after we girls had got off the bus and he had checked in with us: "How did you do on that history test?" Then, after a pause for an answer from me, "How did Harold do?"

I am certain that I have romanticized my father's role in our family over the decades; it is inevitable when one loses someone too young. In recent years, however, I have often read about the evolution of the human conceptualization of God the Father—for example, Richard Rohr's belief that traditional Christianity has all but destroyed the human longing for God with its emphasis on a vengeful, punitive God and a religion of "shoulds." A girl's early image of God the Father is undoubtedly influenced by her own father, his innate ability to love, his notion of the basic human right to wrestle with religion's rules. Somewhere along the way I learned that religion was negotiable. This lesson has kept me in the church, pushing for a more Beloved Community, despite its institutional failures.

I have not emphasized here my adolescent battles with my father, my almost Oedipal need to dethrone him as I sought my own independence. We were both strong willed, and I belonged to a new generation of feminists fighting their way out of traditional views about the roles of men and women. I resisted his power and authority over me. I resisted his insistence on traditional religious values when I wanted to throw it all over with my newly acquired education and small window of adult experience. My point here has to do with the face of patriarchy when balanced by unconditional love. When my feminist friends left the church, I stayed, maybe because of my image of a loving, rather than a vengeful, God. Eventually, I would embrace an understanding of the Trinity as emblematic of outpoured love beyond all doctrine.

Of course, my relationship with my father changed as I turned eighteen and left home for college, met my husband (a man in whom I saw my father's integrity), and became a Vietnam War protester and liberal-minded rebel against the church and its traditions. My father did not necessarily approve of my theology or viewpoints, but I felt the reassurance of his love and intellectual respect. We never quit talking, arguing, wrestling for the truth. Both home from graduate school, my husband and I sat at the table and talked with my father for hours about Vietnam or the peace movement or civil rights or some issue tearing at the institutional church. I remember feeling that my father's beliefs were, like ours, being changed by the tenor of the times, as he more strongly embraced pacifism—Eisenhower-like, perhaps, in his awareness of the horrors of war, the potential for an industrial military complex—this man who had personally witnessed the atrocities of Jewish death camps he helped to liberate at the end of World War II.

As a child my bedtime prayer was "Now I lay me down to sleep, / I pray thee Lord my soul to keep. / If I should die before I wake, / I pray thee Lord, my soul to take." It is a prayer designed to stoke a girl's fears about death, her terrors over thoughts of the end of time. I enumerated for God my many fears. Of the Russians, of course. We had been drilled in school for what to do in case of atomic attack; we practised, huddled on the basement steps of our schoolhouse in the dark with our heads covered. When a plane flew over the playground high in the sky during recess, I stopped my play to gaze up high into the sky, wondering how I could ever distinguish between a Russian plane come to drop a bomb and an ordinary American jet.

My most fervent prayer to an all-powerful God, however, was that my father—my protector, security, fountain of love, and constant affirmer—might be spared. When I was a child, Daddy had been involved in a terrible truck wreck just a couple of miles from our house as he returned home from hauling a load of wheat to Liberal. The other driver was killed. "Please, God, anything, but do not take my father," I prayed into my pillow at night. I could not imagine who else in all the world would intuitively understand me. When my father died of a rare pulmonary disease at age fifty-two while I was still in my twenties, I was hollowed out for years. How would I know what I believed without my father's barometer against which to test my belief? How could I recognize my own change without his steadfastness?

His untimely death, so many years ago now, left a hole indeed, a tender place I carry inside always; however, the years have brought me mostly gratitude: for the years my father lived, for the amazing character he was, for his strong ability to make a girl feel loved. Unlike those who live with regret for an untimely loss that leaves them longing to rewind time, that they might somehow redeem something unspoken, there is nothing I needed to tell my father; I have no sense that I should have said a better goodbye. It had all always been said.

MEMORIED WITH THE FEEL

by Elsie K. Neufeld

He would have turned ninety-five on July 16, 2017, the day on which I turned sixty. He was my father, I was his daughter; we loved one another and still do. We weren't close, but neither were we at odds. I called him *Papa*, then Dad.

I cannot tell our story without including his past, about which he first told me in February 1996, the year I interviewed my parents for *The Past inside the Present: A Family Story*. Till then, Mom was the storyteller, not Dad.

Waldemar Klassen and Elsie K. Neufeld: father and daughter. If not for a series of events that *almost* happened, and others that *did* happen, it might have been otherwise.

My father was born in Milaradowka in 1922. In 1924, his parents, Isaak and Anna Klassen, applied for and were denied a visa to immigrate to Canada. Isaak's sister Maria, however, was successful and immigrated to Abbotsford,

British Columbia. It was she and her daughter who would sponsor my Russian Mennonite parents to come to Canada in 1948.

My father was the youngest of eight brothers; the four eldest were born of a different mother, who died at thirty-one. He did not distinguish between half or full siblings.

His early childhood was play, play, and play—inside and outside on a large estate, where servants and two orphaned female cousins helped with chores and the children. My father didn't know that his father, a landowner, was a *Kulak* and that, for this, was at great risk of being arrested, exiled, or worse—lined up along with the entire family and executed by gunfire.

When my father was seven, armed men on horses appeared on the yard and ordered the family outside. They were fortunate to be only ordered off the property. "We weren't permitted to take anything, not even a bucket of potatoes," Dad recalled. He watched one of the soldiers dismount, then strip the *Pelzmantel* off *Vater* Klassen's back and replace it with his own worn, lice-infested coat. When he told me this story, my father was seventy-three years old, but his face was that of a broken-hearted seven-year-old child. I'd never heard the story before. Nor what followed.

His mother, Anna, and the four youngest boys found shelter in Neuendorf. Dad's father went to work in a factory in Zaporozhye where, in exchange for work, he received a bed in a room shared with fifty others and a daily ration of hot water, a few salted herring, and five hundred grams of bread. He saved the bread to give to his wife and three youngest sons. Sometimes the eldest of the boys was sent to fetch it. Occasionally the four of them visited. My father recalled the final visit: "His bed was empty. He had died of hunger. He had already been buried in a pit, a mass grave for workers. We couldn't see him." My father was eleven, his father had been fifty-four, and his mother was forty-six.

When Dad was fourteen, he left home to attend a *Berufsschule* in Zaporozhe, where he learned a trade and worked in an iron foundry. One day, molten steel spilled onto his foot and burned through his asbestos-lined footwear. He was sent home for medical treatment, to where he lived with his mother, now on her own. She had a heart condition, and on the afternoon of February 13, 1943, she had a heart attack. That evening she had another. Mother and son were alone, and he held her in his arms. "I tried," he said as he recounted her last breaths. "I tried to get her to take the *Medizien*." Tears poured down his face as he spoke and demonstrated with his hands how he'd held her, prompted her, "*aber...*"

But. He shook his head as if still in disbelief.

He summoned Mrs. Thiessen, the neighbour, who bathed and dressed his mother. Someone built a casket; someone dug a hole. It was bitterly cold, and the sound of spades hitting frozen ground could be heard throughout the village—and rang forever in his ears. Anna Klassen was buried two days after she died; she was sixty-one years of age. My father was twenty-one.

It was during this medical leave that the Russians retreated from the advancing Germans. The foundry my father had worked in was dismantled, and the workers were ordered to transport the equipment. Had he still been there, Dad would have been included in that trek northward from which most never returned.

Now he was an orphan.

"What were your parents like, Dad?"

Father Klassen was very strict—had to be with eight sons. What he said was law, and the punishment for disobedience was *Pruegel* (thrashing).

"Did you ever get a thrashing?" No.

Mother Klassen, like all women of her time, "*hatte nichts zu sagen*." She had nothing to say. "*Sie war die Untertan*." She was the subject.

In the second year after the German invasion of Neuendorf, my father enlisted in the German army along with numerous Mennonite friends who, like him, perceived the Germans as their saviours. After all, they wore belt buckles inscribed with "*Gott mit uns*" ("God with us") and, equally significantly, permitted the Mennonites to express their beliefs openly and to resume worship services in their church buildings.

My father joined the *Arbeitergruppe* and was put to work as a translator, conveying orders to the Russian captives tasked with rebuilding the bridge over the Dnieper River. He lived in a barrack. Every morning, he joined the others in singing a patriotic German song and then listened to a speech that reinforced the imperative to be loyal. Then, the dilemma: to swear allegiance to Hitler or not. Mennonites were to swear allegiance only to God. "Some Mennonites did it, others did not," said Dad.

Eventually, Dad ended up fighting on the front. My older sister (by six years) recalls Dad showing her a photo of himself, in uniform, seated on a horse. "He was so proud, so proud." I didn't know the photo existed until the interview; it had been stored in a recycled card box in my parents' dresser. I knew, though, that he'd fought in the German army. Once, as a young child, I asked him, "Did you ever kill anyone?" His response? "I was terrified. I planted my rifle into the mud, put my helmet on top, and laid flat on the ground. Then, Pow! Ping!" He chuckled as he said, "The bullets hit my helmet, and they thought they'd killed one."

It was the only time I'd asked. I somehow knew it was a topic to be avoided. Perhaps from observing my dad watching war movies on TV, how he sat on the edge of his seat, chewing his lower lip, present but absent to everything save for the black-and-white images on the screen. He was there, on the battlefield again, alongside those Germans, the despised, the defeated enemy—on TV and in real life. It was there his life might have ended had he not disobeyed his superior's order to ride ahead, to scout out their enemy's whereabouts. Angrily, his superior rode ahead on his horse, and *boom!* One hoof stepped on a mine, and horse and rider were gone. Dad saw it all. That was a story he told me during the interview, though he'd insisted he wouldn't talk about *Krieg*. The war.

Two years earlier, when my brother-in-law suicided with his hunting rifle in his own home, we helped my sister move from that house. My father whispered to me: "*Das stinkt wie im Krieg.*" He said it was an odour one never forgets.

Now, when he told me of the death he had witnessed and had narrowly avoided himself, I had an inkling of the long-term impact of war. The look in his face and eyes when he alluded to that unforgettable odour, and when describing his commanding officer's death, was much different from what I, as a child, had observed in Dad when he killed farm animals. When he'd take his .22 rifle into the barn, press it between the pigs' eyes and pull the trigger, then finish the job with a butcher knife to the throat. When he'd eviscerate the pigs before slicing, grinding, and processing the meat into chops, head cheese, *Leberwurst*, farmer sausage he'd smoke, and ribs, boiled and smothered with hail-coarse salt.

He also used the rifle to kill a steer and, again, the razor-sharp butcher knife to bleed the animal before suspending it high from a ladder in order to dismember it into steaks, liver, and roasts; ground beef for *holopchi* (Ukrainian spelling); *Kotletten*; and bones to flavour borscht and *Rindtsuppe*. The inedible parts were dumped into a deep hole dug in advance in the harvested potato plot. I would follow Dad as he pushed the wheelbarrow across the rutted field, afraid that he might miss the target, and then what? Would the wobbly animal viscera return to life? I peered at the remains until, still glistening, they settled. I kicked dirt overtop, then ran to Dad's side.

Twice a year, Dad also killed roosters and old laying hens withheld from shipping, and culls he found among the new shipment of chicks, identified within weeks after arrival for "failure to thrive"—meaning not worth their keep. He picked them up by the neck with two fingers, did a swift up-and-down half-windmill once, and crack! Neck broken. He tossed them into the tall grass behind the barn, where they lay, yellow eyes wide, beaks frozen open, heads slumped onto folded wings. Crows and feral barn cats picked them to pieces. I watched in horror.

Laying hens and roosters were placed head-first onto a stump between two parallel nails, then beheaded with one fell of a just-sharpened axe. Blood squirted, geyser-like, then slowed to a dribble and leak till the headless critter ceased dancing nearby, ready to be doused in boiled water, defeathered, and broken open to extract heart, liver, and sometimes premature eggs—yolks and white contained in a membrane, but not yet encapsuled in shell.

I watched and helped as I could with small assigned tasks I never considered not doing: plucking feathers, fetching basins, tending the fire, sweeping up blood, wet feathers, and water off the carport floor or the ground nearby. The scent, sight, texture, smell, and taste of it recorded by my senses.

I don't recall ever seeing a look of fear or disgust on my father's face during animal *Schlachten*. If anything, I sensed a kind of celebratory glee, as if it were more play than work. Butcherings were communal occasions that involved three other families—Mom's siblings; none of Dad's brothers came to Canada—and concluded with a celebratory dinner at which Dad brought out a jug of Calona red wine and poured a glass for anyone over the age of thirteen. Everyone ate with gusto, and there was much laughter as the uncles recounted the killing, especially if the animals had resisted and Dad or one of the uncles who assisted had seemed at risk. At evening's end everyone went home with samples of meat.

❧

The story of Dad witnessing his superior being killed in his place was one of only two *Krieg* stories he told me in 1996. "You have no idea, Elsie, what war is," he said. Did he tell me for any other reason than that I'd asked? Was there relief in the telling? How does a person, a young man, take up a rifle and join others his age to march through all seasons' weather, across various wild terrain, knowing a group of like-minded young men, differentiated only by colour of uniform, are advancing from the opposite direction, with the same orders: Shoot to kill.

I cannot imagine. Not the battle, nor living with the memories of battle, *imprinted forever inside*. How to carry a half-decade of war stories to the grave as my father did?

The second story he told me during the interview took place after war's end. He had surrendered and was a prisoner of war in an American camp. He said the Allies were no better than the Germans, that the prisoners were herded, like animals, onto a field encircled with barbed wire, with armed guards watching from stations overhead. "They'd bring a bucket of water and place it before us. Everyone rushed forward, and the bucket tipped over. It was hot; we were so thirsty we drank the water off the ground where it was mixed with blood and piss." At night, the men slept under the sky, clouded or starlit. Prisoners jostled to find a spot in the middle because those on the edge were at risk of being shot if they moved too close to the fence during sleep. In the morning—every morning—the corpses were removed.

My father survived imprisonment. He and a few Mennonite buddies were released on the condition they find work on surrounding farms; Germany had suffered significant male casualties and many farms were now run by widows and mothers without sons.

The war had interrupted many courtships, too, including my parents' (begun in Neuendorf), but neither forgot the other. Through relatives' letter writing, the German Red Cross, and Mennonite Central Committee (MCC), they were reunited in northwest Germany. They married in November 1946, had their first child in 1947, and immigrated to Canada in June 1948, on the ss *Volendam*.

They left Germany in part because they feared repatriation to Russia. But the Promised Land wasn't how they'd imagined it. Dad said if he'd had the means to return to Germany, he'd have done so the day after arriving in the Fraser Valley. He was sent immediately to the strawberry patch, to pick berries—back-breaking work in hot weather. Everyone spoke English; he knew not a word. Then the husband of Cousin Mary, who with her mother, Maria, had sponsored my parents, informed Dad that he would be charging interest on the *Reiseschuld* (travel debt). Mary intervened, forbidding it. But the words had been spoken. The debt was paid three months later with berry- and hops-picking earnings.

For the remainder of his life, my father would pay all bills before their due date. And as soon as he could, he loaned money to family and friends, interest-free, sometimes at a cost to himself. He cried when he told me the story of being informed of owed interest—the first unexpected betrayal (though he wouldn't have articulated it as such; he was too loyal to family, too indebted to their sponsorship). Another soon followed. He cried as he spoke of this betrayal, too. It cut even deeper, as it involved rejection by the church—the Mennonite Brethren (MB) church of which their sponsors were members.

My parents credited God for their survival. Both had grown up conditioned to not speak of the faith of their parents in school; to do so put parents at risk for arrest. But they were confident in their Christian faith. Both were baptized (sprinkled) by a Mennonite General Conference minister in Germany. Now, here in the land of the free, on the first Sunday they attended church with their MB sponsors, all that was called into question. The service ended, and though their hosts stayed seated my parents were asked to get up and wait outside. Communion was about to be served, and as neither could identify a date of "conversion," nor had either been baptized by immersion, they were both deemed unfit to take Communion.

It was raining, but they waited outdoors for their hosts, their means of transportation. Were their faces as wet then as when they told the story of that hour? "*Those* MBS," my father often said during my growing up years, somewhat bitterly. I never knew why until this telling. Writing it here, I'm crying, too. I feel the depths of that spiritual insult. I remember, with amazement, the blessing my parents gave my younger sister in 1982 when she married an MB, and the two of them joined that very church.

⁙ — ⁙

By the spring of 1955 my parents had four children and had purchased a ten-acre farm. Dad continued to work away from home, and he helped Mom evenings and Saturdays with taming the mostly forested land into a working raspberry and chicken farm. Their three-room house, without indoor plumbing, was no longer adequate. In the fall of 1956, my parents built and moved into a *three-bedroom* house on the same property. The full basement was still unfinished, but the move happened just in time.

July 16, 1957. My father arrived at the hospital at the end of his workday as an autobody repairman at Bill Green Motors. A nurse greeted him with, "Congratulations, Mr. Klassen. You have twins!" My father, whose command of English was limited, said thank you and proceeded to the nursery. It was there he discovered the meaning of "twins"—two babies. It was then, he said, that he lost much of his hair. My twin brother weighed in at six pounds; I was just over four. It must have been the disparity in our size that led to the ever-after treatment of me by family, especially Dad, as "little Elsie." The cull. The skinny, often sickly one, though never sick with life-threatening illness.

Our eldest brother, ten at the time, repeatedly asked, "Are you sure they're both ours?" No doubt Dad felt the same. If he'd had the chance to take home only the first-born twin, I would have been left behind. No one— not my mom, not her doctor—had expected twins. My parents' wish for me, I discovered, was merely to survive.

By this time, my almost-sixty-year-old Oma, newly emigrated from Paraguay with her youngest unmarried son, had moved into the vacated house. She was in another cyclical, year-long depression. "She couldn't even boil a pot of potatoes to help me feed the children while Mom was in the hospital," Dad recounted.

Potatoes seemed to be Dad's measure of survival. Not long before his death in 1998, a door-to-door salesman appeared at my parents' home. Mom was out, so Dad answered the knock. The man pointed at his truck, heaped with freshly harvested potatoes. Dad, who grew potatoes in his backyard garden, purchased a fifty-pound sack of potatoes. "Why?" I asked when he showed me the sack as proudly as if it were his own harvest. "Well, some-body had to help him out."

I had seen him do this throughout my childhood when canvassing sales-men appeared at our seldom-used back door, peddling mirror-framed prints of The Last Supper; nature-themed wall hangings; the 1967 *World Book Encyclopedia*; *Uncle Arthur's Bedtime Stories*; brushes and vacuum cleaners—Dad purchased them all.

Evenings, he opened the back door to strangers, who'd begin with "Your neighbour won't help me, so I hope you can." These were drivers who'd run out of gas on Highway 401; it ran parallel to our farm, with only one farm between ours and the dead-end road. Graciously—as if he'd expected them—Dad would nod, put on his cap and jacket, and walk the person to the tank by the barn (car gas on one side; tractor gas on the other) and fill their receptacles. If they had no receptacle, he provided one and asked them to return it; they always did. I can't recall him ever saying no to such requests, but I do recall him being annoyed with the next-door neighbours for not helping. He could understand that the Ficks, the Jehovah Witnesses, didn't, but Isaak? Our Mennonite neighbour? A church deacon!

As generous as he was—my father didn't charge for the gas—he rarely asked for help. He told me of times he had. The first occurred right after they'd moved to the farm. Dad walked to the corner of the street to ask the Russian man living there if he could access his water until he'd dug a well. Mr. Domino declined, but when Dad offered to pay, he changed his mind. "Not even one bucket for free," Dad said. On another occasion he asked my mother's cousin to lend him money. "No. He said no. And I knew he had the money. *Mann's Kerl*," he said, shaking his head. Not an expression that can be adequately translated. The tone in his voice was a mix of exasperation, confusion, and lingering humiliation. For as long as I knew my father, he was generous, without prejudice. Sometimes to a fault. The money loaned to others was not always returned. He didn't pursue it.

Like him, I rarely ask for help. The Bible verse "It is more blessed to give than to receive" resonates (Acts 20:35).

My first memory of Dad is aural. My father's low voice wends its way down the hallway into my darkened bedroom where I am falling asleep. It is muted, slightly tremulous, but monotone, not melodious. Comforting. He is reading a passage from *Die Heilige Schrift*, as he does nightly, to Mom. Sometimes my twin and I sneak into Mom and Dad's bedroom, slide open the headboard, and look inside. The Bible is heavy, too heavy to lift, so I slide it onto the white chenille bedspread. Its hard black covers wiggle, and the worn spine is thready. The pages are onion-skin airy, sound crisp when turned, and the page ends are raspberry red, just like the limp ribbon marker dangling out the bottom. It feels like we've trespassed onto holy ground.

Dad doesn't read the Bible aloud to the family. The only time we hear the Bible read is on Sunday mornings, seated in the cavernous West Abbotsford General Conference Mennonite church with its seemingly heaven-high ceiling. The amplified voice travels from the distant pulpit on stage. At the end of the service, *Aeltester* A.A. Harder raises both hands and, in a very loud voice that warbles—rises and falls like a quilt being shook out before covering a bed—recites "*Der Herr Segne Dich und behuete dich....*" The Lord bless you and keep you. I lift my head, listen and watch, terrified and awed. He's so different than Dad.

My father never prays aloud at home either. At bedtime, it's mostly Mom who stands at my bedside while I kneel on my bed to recite first a Low German prayer in which I ask Baby Jesus to build a permanent home in my heart and then a High German prayer imploring God to make me humble enough to get into heaven. Occasionally, it is my father who stands at my bedside. I have no memory of Dad hugging or kissing me goodnight; we shake hands, he says "*Gute Nacht*," then the light goes off.

At meals, Dad is the first to bow his head, and we children recite "*Segne Vater diese Speise.*" In high school and beyond, everyone prays "in their heads." I zoom through *Segne Vater* in my head and keep my head down until Dad clears his throat—the signal to eat. Only in later years, at family gatherings, will my father recite *"Komm Herr Jesu, seih du unser Gast, und segne was Du uns bescheeret hast."* Come Lord Jesus, be our guest....I love the sound of his voice. It is casual, yet reverent.

My father rarely speaks of his faith, but we attend church every Sunday morning. The day before, on Saturday, everyone takes their weekly bath. Oma first, then us young children. Dad waits until after supper to give the hot water tank time to refill. He doesn't share his water. Nor does he hurry. Sometimes he falls asleep; his snores can be heard down the hallway and into the basement. At some point he'll call, "Sus. Sus!" Mom takes a bobby pin from her hair and pokes it into the doorknob to unlock the bathroom door. The sounds change: running tap water; splashing; a noisy *Rutsch* as Dad sits up; soft murmurs as Mom scrubs Dad's back with the long-handled pink bath brush we all use. When Mom emerges, she locks the door from the inside. This may or may not mark the end of Dad's bath. If it takes much longer, Mom herself *puttahs* on the door, and calls out, "Waldemar!"

When Dad emerges, thick steam escapes in two directions: billowing into the hallway and through the screen of the opened window. Dad's *Arbeitskleider* (work clothes) lie heaped on the floor. Mom will remove those later, after he emerges in clean boxers and a white undershirt she'd brought in earlier. The empty tub has a ring around it that she erases with a rag sprinkled with Comet. It looks like the sweat-ring on Dad's cap after a day of picking raspberries.

Dad has a big bald spot. His head resembles a clown's, bald on top with a fringe of hair all around—grey, though, not orange. A scant tuft of hair remains near his forehead, and those strands are long! I don't recall at what age it started or stopped, but sometimes I stand behind his chair after dinner and play with that hair. I slide the individual hairs up through my fingers— from root to tip—to measure their length, then stroke them flat, tips merged with the fringe of remaining hair. Enough to go for regular haircuts. I am mesmerized; it feels almost hypnotic, and he seems to enjoy it as much as I do. My fingers are memoried with the feel of his hair, with the warmth and smoothness of his bald spot. (My daughter would do the same; indeed, she did this spontaneously at my father's viewing, surprised at how cold he was.)

On some Saturday evenings, the stance reverses. I climb onto the high chair, up its two steps that squeal when let down or folded back. Dad stands before me with scissors, a small black pocket comb, and a white cape to drape round my shoulders. I squinch my eyes shut as hard as I can while he wets my bangs with water he takes from a glass, flattens them on my forehead, then snips a straight line. My nose and cheeks tickle. He swishes a brush across my face afterward, then blows away the stragglers. His breath smells like peppermint and the faint smell of something else.

Sometimes I have to use the toilet before Mom cleans the bathroom after Dad's bath. The room smells of Ivory soap, and Dad's barn clothes, which lie on the floor, and a faint scent of...smoke? As I watch the steam from his bath rush out the window, I tiptoe to look out. There, on the ledge between sill and screen, lies the source of "something else": ashes. Cigarette ashes. My father is a closet smoker; it seems like I have known it all my life.

We don't speak of such matters at home, but I have acquired the knowledge of good and evil in church on Sunday mornings (and later, in the private Mennonite high school), so I know that smoking is a sin. And that's probably why he covers it up, and we all help him keep the secret.

Although my father is not involved in kitchen tasks (that's Mom's and daughters' domain), the corner cupboard is Dad's *Schrank*. Inside are his haircutting scissors and comb; his electric *Razieroperat* (he shaves mornings and after dinner); a bottle of Aqua Velva or Old Spice; and a bag of Scotch mints. The aftershave and mints help cover the scent of his sin. I've seen his packet of Players up close, too—in the pocket of his work pants that hang in his *Huehnerkleiderschrank* in the hall. There's always a telltale bulge in his pants pocket, too. Never in church pants, though; *never* in church pants. There are, however, as always, Scotch mints in his Sunday pants—at the ready for him and to share with us on the way to or from church.

Dad smokes out the bathroom window every day, and in the barn, too, where, when caught, he tosses the lit cigarette, lightning quick, into the manure under the cages and coughs to cover his embarrassment for getting caught. I try to warn him by singing or whistling as I approach, but he doesn't always hear me. Only in adulthood do we siblings talk about the ways each of us devised to warn him. To protect him (and ourselves?) from the embarrassment of his knowing we know. No one recalls talking directly to him, although it's said that John, who died, once offered Dad one of his smokes. Dad declined. And once, our younger sister, upon seeing Dad set fire to a nest of *Raupen* on the plum tree with his cigarette lighter, asked, "Papa, do you smoke?" "Sometimes," he replied.

When Dad picks us up after school on rainy days, the car always smells of smoke. He never smokes in the car on Friday nights, though; that's the night he drives Mom and Oma to Clearbrook to do their shopping. Mom doesn't have her licence.

Dad loves cars, and he loves driving. In 1967, he came home with a brand new aubergine Pontiac Parisienne. He hadn't (nor ever would have) consulted Mom. That summer we drove to Winnipeg to visit relatives. Out of the blue, while on the highway, Dad smoked! He didn't make eye contact with any of us, just opened the power window on his side, lit a cigarette, and exhaled. Mom, as if this were not normally kept hidden, turned to the back and announced, "Dad said he has to smoke to keep from falling asleep while driving." It was a three-day journey, but that's the only time I recall him smoking in front of us children. In Winnipeg, I inadvertently saw him smoke in the backyard with an uncle; no one said a word.

The Pontiac was a different matter. All the uncles and cousins surrounded the car and watched Dad show off the power windows and listened to him boast about the power steering and brakes. The uncles and older boy cousins oohed and aahed. Dad grinned proudly, and I felt proud, too.

On the return trip, Dad drove from Winnipeg to Banff without stopping. He loved driving, and even though the new car had power steering, he gripped the wheel as if it didn't, turning the wheel slightly left and then to the right, then again left, as if it needed correction.

It was near midnight when we arrived in Banff, and I'd fallen asleep. Dad picked me up from the back seat and carried me into the motel room. I was half-awake, but pretended to be fully asleep. I did that other times, too, when we'd come home late from visiting relatives—feign sleep in order to be held by my father, who wasn't otherwise physically affectionate.

As for the smoking, he never again smoked while driving with us in the car. And it was Mom, not Dad, who told me when he quit, cold turkey, in 1986. He was scheduled for gall bladder surgery, and a cousin had told him that being a smoker put him at risk for post-op complications, so he quit.

Just like that. One of my biggest regrets is not acknowledging that. So, I say it here: Dad, I'm proud you could quit. And it wasn't—it wasn't!—a sin. I wish I'd had the courage to say so then. With a hug!

⁂

Try as I might I can't recall as a child ever sitting on Dad's lap, or hugging him. I imagine I held his hand (does any child *not* hold her father's hand?), but no specific memory comes to mind. There wasn't discomfort in being physically close, although there was a hint as I grew older that Dad wasn't at ease with his daughters maturing physically into women. I was sixteen and had come to lunch wearing a bikini. Afterward, Mom took me aside and said, "Dad doesn't want you to come to the table in your bathing suit." I was stunned. I hadn't given it a second thought. No explanation was given. I felt shame. I wanted to vanish. Years later, at a family gathering when I pulled up my top to show my brother my pregnant belly, my father blushed and looked away.

I'm not sure why these memories converge here on the page—perhaps to appease some hurt felt then upon knowing, albeit subconsciously, that an ease between us had ended. I suddenly felt a self-consciousness around him that I can't recall having experienced before then. It was confusing. Writing this, I feel an even greater need for a specific memory to confirm that it wasn't always so. And then my body remembers: I snuggled with Dad. Uninhibited.

I am a preschooler, in our West Abbotsford church.

Women and men sat divided. I pester and pull on Mom's sleeve, beg to go sit with *Papa*. "*Nein. Sitz still,*" she whispers. She brushes my hand away. I persist till she relents, then tiptoe across the carpeted aisle.

I sit on Dad's right side. My head leans against his shoulder, and I tuck into his side. I can smell him and hear his breathing; I can feel the rise and fall of his chest on my arm, we're seated that close. There is no more to this memory than that: it's just Dad and me, arms melded. I may have put my hand into his jacket pocket and helped myself to a Scotch mint tainted with Aqua Velva. I may not have. All I know is that the moment was perfect, so perfect that it might have been only a father and daughter—we two—alone in a sanctuary that accommodated six hundred.

Back home, I sit on my bedroom floor, crack leftover Christmas peanuts from their shells. *"Elsie, komm her,"* calls my mother from her bedroom. To my surprise, she is holding her slipper in hand when I enter, and beckons me to lie on the bed. "Next time you will sit still in church," she says in German. *"Nicht. Mehr. Vribblen. In die Kirche."*

It wasn't the last time I sat with Dad in church, but it is my sole memory of sitting with him in that church. Close. So close. I couldn't have sat any closer or I'd have disappeared.

⁂

In 1963, our family joined a new church that my parents helped found: Eben-Ezer. The split happened because a small group of Russian Mennonite immigrants wanted to retain German-language services, including Sunday school.

As busy as Dad was at home as a full-time farmer, and with a seventh child, he always had a volunteer job at church. For a while he was an usher and sat in the foyer with the other *Platzanweisers.* My Uncle George, a successful businessman, was an usher, too. Sometimes Uncle George beckoned me over, and I'd go sit near the large window through which you could view the entire congregation from the back. Once, I overheard him saying something to another usher about *"Kolkopps"* as the two of them stood by the window, whispering. I sat, looking up at them. My uncle pointed, swept his hand across the men's section, chuckled, and added something about *"blitzblank en jlitzrich."* Shiny and glittering.

Their laughter sounded derogatory, and it felt as though they were laughing at Dad, who, like the other men my uncle pointed at, had a balding head that glistened under the lights. I felt something akin to shame, and also wanted to protect my dad, so I hurried back to his side. I watched the ushers go forward for the offering, tracked the way my father gave and received the black velvet *Beutel* from hands of people seated at the end at each row. I was proud, but also a little sad about my uncle's comment. It didn't feel right.

One year Dad agreed to take on the job of overseeing the sound system. Someone must have shown him how to manage the soundboard to control the microphones at the front, but they often squealed and screeched so loud that people visibly startled. Dad squirmed and fiddled with knobs, turned this one and that. I sat, anxiously, watching till the only sound was the clear voice of the speaker. The job was twofold; Dad also looked after the suit-case-sized tape recorder. It travelled to and from church in the trunk of the car. So many buttons! Record; Play; Rewind. The twin spools on which the thin brown tape travelled were almost as large as dinner plates; they whirred and hummed. I got lost in the watching.

Dad took his job seriously. He stopped the machine whenever the congregation rose, started it again when the pastor prayed, then turned it off again as people sat down, then on again once everyone was seated. Was it my anxiety or his that I felt as I watched to make sure he pushed Record, then fiddled with dials while a tiny green needle see-sawed inside a plastic-sealed compartment? I stayed seated with him as the congregation dispersed, the two of us watching the reel on the right side empty its tape onto the left. The reel on rewind made a high-pitched *eeeee*, and the tape flew faster and faster. Occasionally it exceeded the capacity of what the opposite reel could accept, and the brown tape ballooned sideways. Dad fumbled with the off button and slowly, carefully, manually wound the tape onto the receiving spool. Something in the way he did it signalled possible trouble, and I kept watch as if doing so would help avoid disaster.

It was on Sunday afternoons that my father's talent for quiet companionship was revealed. I didn't know till writing this how much I learned from him of how to *be with* people. For that's what he was doing when he delivered the taped service to members unable to attend church in the morning. Mr. Bergen on Church Road was one. He was pale, and shorter than most men—skinny, too, like a child, light as a hollowed tree that a sudden wind might topple. He lived alone in a tiny house that seemed as frail and decrepit as he. (In the early 1970s, after an incident involving a boy and the police, he would confess to the pastor, who brought it to the congregation and proposed he be forgiven—and he was, by a show of hands.) I accompanied Dad to his house only once.

On several occasions I went with Dad to visit the Giesbrechts, who lived in a long-in-the-tooth house on Queens Road—the same road our pastor lived on. The stairs to the back door were steep and rickety. Mrs. Giesbrecht was pumpkin round and taller than her thin, bent husband, who wore suspenders to keep his pants up. Her hair was unkempt and their house reeked of oil heat, cabbage, and mildew. Mr. Giesbrecht had a grey moustache and bottle-brush eyebrows. When he attended church, he sat at the front in the men's section, a *Hoerapparat* that resembled a telephone receiver pressed against his ear, a cord running between it and the pew before him. When Mr. Giesbrecht answered the door, my father shouted, "*Goondach, Onkel Yiesbracht*" and shook his hand with a grin.

Inside the living room, Dad removed his church hat, placed the recorder on a table, fiddled awhile, then pressed Play. We three sat back. Mrs. Giesbrecht sat in the kitchen. My father listened intently, as if hearing it for the first time. Mr. Giesbrecht pointed at a bowlful of candy and motioned me to help myself. Dad did too. We sucked hard candies while Dad rewound the tape, shook Mr. Giesbrecht's hand again, and from the outside stairs wished him *Goodenowent*.

My parents often visited the elderly, the sick, and people whom Mom said "*liegt auf Sterben*." The dying. My twin brother and I went along to viewings, which happened on weekday evenings. The drive there was silent and sombre, but the drive home often included comments about how thin the person was or, when Dad's *Tante* Greta died, how much makeup she had on (too much!). Not one word was said about what we'd see or had seen. It was like going to church, only with far fewer people, and an organ played in the background, not a piano.

Funerals from my childhood blur together as a murder of crows—everyone dressed in black, and women wailing. "*Herzliches Beileid*," my father would say as he shook the hands of the mourning family members lined up to receive condolences. Tears ran down his face, and he chewed on his lip during the service. If Dad was a pallbearer, as at *Onkel* David Funk's *Begraebnis* (funeral), he wore a black armband over the upper left sleeve of his church suit. Afterward, the band lay on my parents' dresser, like sadness made tangible. Seeing it made me feel like I did when I peeked at Dad's face in church, when Mom rose on the women's side during the communal sharing and prayer and wept as she talked about "*die Flucht, und Hungersnot... und wie hat mein Vater zu denn Herr geschrien*." ("The Great Trek, famine... and how Father cried out to God.") Dad sat still as a nailhead, tears running down his face, *plop-plopping* onto his jacket and thighs. He didn't wipe them away. My stomach felt sick. No one spoke on the way home from church.

⁂

My father wasn't strict with me. He never spanked me. Perhaps it was for that reason that I felt thoroughly humiliated the year he reprimanded me.

In church I sang in a children's choir. Mrs. T, the *Prediger*'s wife, was the conductor. She was thin, flat-chested, barren, and wore formless shifts—dresses that resembled girls' nightgowns. She didn't interact with the women in the church. Except for teaching a few piano students and leading both church choirs, she was reclusive. She and the minister lived in a three-room house in a forest; it had no indoor toilet. Everyone knew she didn't cook, sew, or bake, and that her husband went out to eat in restaurants or was invited to dine at parishioners'.

She was bossy and a perfectionist. When displeased with our singing, her neck turned blotchy, her lips pinched together, and the baton in her hand jabbed at the air. "*Langsam, laut, und klar!*" she'd shriek. Slowly, loudly, clearly! To those who couldn't carry a tune—like my first cousin Leona, or the Hildebrandt boys, who were all cognitively challenged—she suggested, within earshot of all, that they only mouth, not sing, the words. She also made them sit at the back, or on the side behind the piano.

It happened that I had a good voice and thus was favoured. I sang duets with my twin and often recited poems from memory. I was also acutely sensitive and noticed her unfair, even demeaning, treatment of children. It irked me. I mentioned this to my parents, who seemed in agreement but dismissed her manner with "that's just how she is." There was also mention of her having no children. A tone of pity.

One Sunday morning, the *Kinderchor* (children's choir) was summoned to the youth room in the church basement for an extra practice; the annual summertime *Kinderfest* (children's festival) was imminent and some choir members still hadn't memorized the melodies or the lyrics. I was eleven, almost twelve, and knew both. Mrs. T pointed her baton at me and said, "You will sing the second verse solo."

"No," I said, quietly.

"What did you say?" she asked.

"I said no."

"You don't want to sing a solo?" she asked, her neck and jaw splotched red, her voice baby-bird squeaky.

"No," I repeated.

Her face darkened, and in a sulky voice she said, "Well. Okay, then." She turned away abruptly, pointed at someone else, and said, "You'll do it, won't you." That girl nodded.

I sat stunned—surprised at what I had done and at Mrs. T's reaction. I was certain, however, that my parents would understand, so as soon as I got into the car I blurted out, "That Mrs. T—she is so stupid. You won't believe what she did. She never asks, she always tells us what to do."

Silence.

My parents looked at each other in the front seat, and then Dad looked at me in the rear-view mirror. "You did what?"

I repeated my grievance. Silence followed.

At home, my father took me aside and gave me two options: (1) a spanking for not complying, or (2) a phone call to Mrs. T with an apology and a change of mind.

I didn't think long; I muttered that I'd call her. I went into the hall where the telephone hung on the wall, turned on the light, closed all the hallway doors so no one would hear me, and with church directory in hand, dialed Mrs. T's phone number.

She answered, her voice high and then higher when I stated my name. Weeping, I apologized, and said I'd sing the solo. She accepted the apology, but refused my offer to sing. Still weeping, I rushed to my bedroom and, mortified, sobbed into my pillow.

Soon my father entered the room. Sternly, he asked if I'd made the call. I mumbled "*Ja*" into my pillow. Then he told me to stop crying—lunch was ready and I was to come to the table.

At *Kinderfest* I stood on the log "stage" in Dunach Park and sang every song from memory. I avoided eye contact with Mrs. T, looked past her, into the audience. I watched, with slight chagrin, as the other girl sang the solo. My eye caught sight of my parents, sitting with my visiting Manitoba relatives. How, I wondered, would it have felt if I'd been standing behind the microphone, singing the solo?

That was the only time to my memory that my father punished me. He needn't have.

Kinderfest that year was memorable not only because of the solo I didn't sing. That afternoon, our family gathered in the living room around the RCA television. It was July 20, 1969, and that day the first man walked on the moon.

Unlike my sisters—one six years older, the other six years younger—I never had a penchant or passion for cooking, baking, sewing, and entertaining. My father noted this early on.

I think I was in junior high when he asked me to serve him lunch. I set the table, then brought over pork and beans (I think), but they hadn't been heated through. As I opened the fridge door to take out the milk, he said to my mother, who stood by the stove, "Can't you teach her anything?" I was still standing by the fridge, looking in, hearing his voice.

On another occasion, in the spring of 1985 when I was already the mother of two rambunctious sons, Dad stopped by to find the house a mess and my boys running wild in the neighbourhood. I was completing a writing assignment, I explained. He questioned my spending my time in such manner.

"What am I supposed to do, Dad? It's boring being at home with two kids."

"Why don't you take a knitting class?" he said, in all seriousness. Did I or did I not tell him I'd tried and failed at that, too? That I was a knitting course dropout; the frustration of repeatedly finding my practice swatches unravelled by my sons and the humiliation in being unable to hold my thumbs and yarn just so in class were good reasons to quit.

Neither of us knew where that writing course would take me—how, two years later, I'd write my way through the grief of my brother John's death; win two honorary awards for my first-ever published essay, entitled "Who Is My Neighbour?"; and go on to publish my first non-fiction book, *Dancing in the Dark: A Sister Grieves.**

---

*   Elsie K. Neufeld, *Dancing in the Dark: A Sister Grieves* (Scottdale, PA: Herald Press, 1990).

Nor did either of us imagine that ten years after Dad advised me to take up knitting, I'd interview him and Mom and write a book about their lives. A book he'd proudly gift to his children for Christmas that year. A book dedicated to his children, grandchildren, and those yet to come.

The experience of interviewing my parents was inexplicably profound. I now saw my parents as persons—ordinary persons with extraordinary stories. I wanted others to experience the wonder of recording their story or that of another family, and I resolved to teach them how. This led to fifteen years of teaching in venues throughout the Fraser Valley and Lower Mainland—at Fraser Valley College (now UFV), in Learning Plus programs, in hospices, for non-profit organizations, and at all manner of conferences. In every setting, I referred to my parents' story and how hearing their stories enhanced our relationship as person to person, not only parent and child. Eventually, I became a personal historian and a eulogist. From my mother I learned how to tell stories; from my father I learned how to sit quietly and listen. If only to silence. That is their legacy.

My father, Waldemar Klassen, died at age seventy-five, twenty-two hours after suffering a massive stroke. There had been time enough to squeeze his hand, and he squeezed back, his left eye leaking tears, before he went into a coma.

Tuesday, April 14, 1998. Our family gathers in a tiny hospital room around his *Leiche*, his body, and take turns saying farewell. It's 4:30 a.m. A single yellowish light illumines his face. Outside, dawn is brush-stroking the sky with light and the far mountains turn pink.

My parents' minister, a conservative Mennonite Brethren man who is only an interim minister at their General Conference church, had asked to be called. Someone does. I can't be objective or receptive.

In the previous year, my twin brother came out as gay. When I go to be with my parents after my brother has told them, only my father is home. He is disconsolate. Tells me the minister has been to visit, at my parents' request. My father weeps; it is heart-rending. "Here I asked him to come, hoped he would comfort us"—he speaks German, uses the word *troesten*—"and he reads verses from the Bible that say homosexuals will go to hell." He shakes his head in wonder. In anger. I tell him the man failed him. And that he's wrong. That the Bible also says that "nothing can separate us from the love of God" (Rom. 8:38). That love is all that matters.

I think of that conversation when this same minister arrives now, when he enters the hospital room like a shadow preceding a man. Brings darkness, disguised as light. "Absent in body, present with the Lord," he quips, almost cheerfully.

My writer-self is amused; my daughter-self wants to scream, "How dare you? He's still present!" Dad's right bear-paw hand is cradled between mine; it's still warm. It glistens with my tears as I kiss it, hold it to my cheek, and tell him, inside my head—certain he hears me—that I love him, will miss him, and am so glad his wish is fulfilled. He won't end life in a wheelchair—diapered, drooling, and dependent. That was his biggest fear, expressed often.

During the next days, as we prepare for Dad's funeral, this minister continues to effuse maddening clichés, most often "May God be glorified." He speaks as if absent from our reality: that we are in mourning. He doesn't acknowledge this even once. Nothing he says comforts; it all rankles. Our father did not use the minister's choice of language, ever. Dad lived, not spoke, his faith. My daughter, ten, astutely observes, "Mommy, why does that man keep saying those weird things?" When I tell my mother how Dad would have hated this language, she agrees, yet excuses the minister with "that's just how he talks." Thankfully, his only task at the service will be reading Scripture selected by us.

My "absent in body" father remains present as I write his eulogy, when we sing during the service, and at the cemetery where we stand at the edge of his grave—a robin singing from a treetop during the readings and prayers. Everyone notices, and speaks of it later.

If spirits of our beloved dead manifest themselves in creaturely form, I'm certain that bird is my brother, who died eleven years earlier and is buried a stone's throw from where we stand. Now, as we lay our father to rest, it seems our brother is whistling our father home in the same way Dad used to whistle us home from our play in the nearby forest and pond at chore time.

In the week following Dad's death, I continue to feel Dad's presence.

We siblings gather in our parents' home, to divide Dad's things—peacefully, generously—often deferring to one another about an item, with "I think you should have this." I take a cap, for Dad was never without a hat. He had everyday caps and Sunday hats: black for winter, grey for summer.

All is organized, and Dad would be proud of the display, categorized as if a library: hats here; belts there; socks, ties, and undershirts, all neatly displayed on the pool table. Shoes lined on the floor: good shoes, leather, in multiple colours, polished shiny, as if he knew. Jackets, shirts, and Sunday suits on a line strung between opposite walls. A black leather jacket he'd worn only once.

Worn only once? Mom explains that the first time he'd worn it, her brother had commented, laughingly, "You look just like a Nazi." The jacket was put at the back of the closet and only revealed to us all on this day. It's the first time I've heard that story.

Whatever is left of the clothes will go to MCC, as Dad would have wanted it, as he himself would have done it. The same will go for the tools.

The garage has been emptied of the car and truck in order to display Dad's tools on the floor, walls, and tables—one is makeshift, of plywood atop two sawhorses. In childhood my twin and I used to set it up just so, with orange crates beneath to serve as seats, an old tricycle wheel hammered onto the left leg of the sawhorse, a stick on the left to turn on the pretend signal light. This was our "car." The driver—most often me—inserted the pretend key into the pretend ignition, then steered the wheel left and right like Dad always did, and shifted the "gear-stick" from park into drive. We both made car noises. What fun we had as we pretend-travelled to places Dad took us to in real life: to Swans' Point, Cultus Lake, Keremeos; to Army & Navy in New Westminster; to church—places we'd drive to ourselves when we acquired our own driver's licences.

Dad taught us all how to drive, and he paid half the cost of a blue VW we twins purchased together. The day before my driver's test, my older brother, a truck driver, unexpectedly came home. Dad asked him to take me out for a last "test" drive. My brother said I wouldn't pass as I couldn't park properly, but I declared I would. I hoped I'd not be assigned the examiner with the reputation for failing everyone, but that's who I got. He had a brush cut and a scowl on his face, and said little. "Right here." "Left at the stop sign." "Park up the hill." Not only did I park too far from the curb, and turn the wheel incorrectly, but I also nearly hit a pedestrian on a crosswalk. The examiner declared the test over and instructed me to return to the Bureau. Dad sat inside, waiting. I looked at him and burst into tears. He pulled his handkerchief out of his pocket and handed it to me. In the car, he turned the ignition and said, "I knew as soon as I saw that man, that he'd fail you." After that, Dad sent me to driving school for a one-hour session; I redid the test with their much-smaller car and passed.

These are the kinds of stories we siblings remember as we divide Dad's things. It's Father's Day, 1998, and he is present with us in as close a manner as one can be after death. Close on this day, and closer later.

In 2010, my left breast springs a leak—as I'm writing! I am fast-tracked for a mammogram, ultrasound, and biopsy.

Carcinoma in situ? My doctor thinks so, but doesn't tell me until later. From stained T-shirt to surgery is less than two weeks.

Then I wait for the biopsy results.

One afternoon, I fall asleep on the couch. A knock sounds at the door. I get up and find my father there. He declines my invitation to come in. He stands in the hallway, tells me not to worry, that the biopsy will not reveal cancer. We look at each other. Then he vanishes.

I immediately share the experience by email with a good friend, who too has told me all will be well. And I want a record of what just occurred.

The excised lump and duct are benign. Who can explain such things? I don't need an explanation.

"*Lieber Vater, hoch im Himmel, merk auf deines Kinderlein....*"

"Loving Father in heaven, remember your little children."

CONTRIBUTOR BIOGRAPHIES

Carol Dyck (**née Voth**) grew up in Saskatoon, Saskatchewan, and now lives in Edmonton, Alberta. She has been a teacher, a professional chorister, a choral conductor, a church musician, and a composer of solo and choral music. She has composed four larger works for solos and choir, one of which, *Every Deliverance*, was performed at a Mennonite World Conference in Strasbourg, France.

Maggie Dyck was born and bred on the Alberta prairie. She studied music in Winnipeg and Germany and earned a degree in art history at the University of Waterloo. She is a singer, an arts tour coordinator, a writer, a wife, a mother, and a grandmother. She and her husband, Howard Dyck, live in Waterloo, Ontario.

Raylene Hinz-Penner was born and raised on the soil of the southwest Kansas/Oklahoma Panhandle border in the US Midwest, accounting for her interest in "place," especially geographic and human-designed borders shaped over time. Her passion in life is teaching literature and composition of all forms, leading her to writing projects that refuse to maintain clean genre borders, instead blurring non-fiction forms: memoir, prose poem, and essay. Her favourite place today is somewhere in the Kansas Flint Hills not far from Topeka, where she lives with her husband, Doug.

Ann Hostetler is the author of a volume of poetry, *Empty Room with Light*, and the editor of *A Cappella: Mennonite Voices in Poetry*. Her second book of poems, *Safehold*, will be published in fall 2018. She is the editor of the Center for Mennonite Writing's website (www.mennonitewriting.org) and co-editor of the *Journal of Mennonite Writing*. She teaches English and creative writing at Goshen College in Goshen, Indiana.

Jean Janzen was born in Saskatchewan and raised in the American Midwest; she moved in 1957 to California, where her husband practised pediatrics and where together they raised four children. She graduated from Fresno Pacific University and studied poetry during graduate work at Fresno State University. She has published seven books of poetry, two books of essays, and hymn texts in the Mennonite Hymnal.

Lynda Loewen was born and raised in small-town Manitoba. She and her husband and two teenage girls now live in a spot in Winnipeg that feels like a small town. Her work life has been devoted to puzzling through the rough patches with individuals and families, first as a social worker and then as a marriage and family therapist. She also teaches psychology at Canadian Mennonite University.

Mary Ann Loewen was born in Lincoln, Nebraska, but has spent most of her life in Manitoba, Canada. She spent a few years working as a nurse, then taught piano part-time when her kids were young, and then realized that she wanted to know more about reading and writing. Since her stint in grad school, she has taught academic writing at the University of Winnipeg, and Canadian literature at Canadian Mennonite University. She loves spending time in her kitchen and hanging out with her family: her husband, three adult children, and one adorable grandson.

Ruth Loewen was born and mostly raised in Manitoba, but has lived in Ontario for much of her adult life. Her career has included research on various topics, such as sensory testing, food preferences in childhood, memory in aging, and, currently, tobacco use. She works for a small but influential research group at the University of Waterloo, the International Tobacco Control (ITC) Project, which conducts surveys in many countries to investigate effective anti-tobacco policies. She is an avid quilter, a member of several book clubs, and the occasionally grudging servant of two cats.

Elsie K. Neufeld is a poet, editor, eulogist, and also a personal historian who has midwifed twenty books into being. Her primary work these days is the corporate history of Mott Electric, a fourth-generation family-owned business that began in 1930. Elsie lives in Vancouver's West End, where she enjoys walks, photography, live blues music, and volunteering in the West End Seniors Thrift Store. She has three children, with a grandchild on the way.

Cari Penner is deputy mayor of, and a strong advocate for, the City of Steinbach, as well as a wife, mother, and proud grandma. The first woman to be elected to municipal politics in her community, she enjoys exploring the intricacies of zoning by-laws, municipal policies, and development plans. Although many still find this peculiar, she argues that the traditional *Fruehes* pursuits of cooking and cleaning are just part of what makes a great city.

Rebecca Plett is a cultural anthropologist whose work focuses on Mennonite affect and identity and has been published in several academic journals. Having grown up in southern Manitoba, she currently lives, writes, and teaches in beautiful Hamilton, Ontario.

Magdalene Redekop was born in Winkler, Manitoba, and grew up on a farm halfway between Rosenfeld and Altona. She is Professor Emerita at the University of Toronto, where she taught courses on comedy and Canadian literature. Magdalene enjoys being a grandmother, doing jigsaw puzzles, and watching movies with her husband. Since retirement she has been at work on a book entitled *Making Believe: Mennonites Looking for Spielraum*.

Carrie Snyder, after a peripatetic childhood, is happily settled with her family in Waterloo, Ontario, where she lives near most of her four younger siblings and both of her parents. She is the author of three books for adults, including *Girl Runner*, which has been translated into twelve languages, and *The Juliet Stories*, a finalist for a Governor General's Award. Carrie also teaches creative writing at the University of Waterloo. For her latest project, she is drawing cartoons—because not everything can be expressed in words.

Julia Spicher Kasdorf was born in Lewistown, in what is now the second poorest county in the Commonwealth of Pennsylvania due to outmigration, demise of family farms, and the cash-poor alternate economy of the Anabaptist sectarians, she speculates. Author of four collections of poetry, a book of essays, and a biography of Joseph W. Yoder, she writes locally and thinks historically while teaching creative writing at Penn State. *Shale Play*, a book of poems by Spicher Kasdorf with photographs by Steven Rubin documenting the human and environmental impacts of fracking in Pennsylvania, is forthcoming in 2018 from Penn State Press. She has also begun work on a biography of Alta Elizabeth Schrock (1919–2001), the Amish-born Appalachian ecologist and humanitarian, and the first woman to earn a PhD (University of Pittsburgh, biology, 1944) and remain in the Mennonite Church. She lives with her husband, Philip Ruth, and a daughter in Bellefonte, Pennsylvania.

Hildi Froese Tiessen grew up near the Red River in East Kildonan, Winnipeg. A graduate of Mennonite Brethren Collegiate Institute and the Universities of Winnipeg and Alberta, she taught English literature and film studies at Wilfrid Laurier University before moving to Conrad Grebel University College at the University of Waterloo. Hildi has published articles on Mennonite literature, curated/edited volumes of work by and about Mennonite writers, and co-organized numerous international conferences entitled "Mennonite/s Writing"; she and her husband, Paul, have published a number of books together, including volumes focused on the work of artists of Mennonite descent. Hildi and Paul live in Kitchener, where they always look forward to visits with their two sons and their families.